Cyber Security

This Book Includes:

Hacking with Kali Linux,

Ethical Hacking.

*Learn How to Manage Cyber Risks Using
Defense Strategies and Penetration Testing for
Information Systems Security*

Zach Codings

Table of Contents

Hacking with Kali Linux

Ethical Hacking

Hacking with Kali Linux

A Beginner's Guide to Learn Penetration Testing to Protect Your Family and Business from Cyber Attacks Building a Home Security System for Wireless Network Security

Zach Codings

Introduction

The first recorded incident of hacking happened back in the 1960s at the Massachusetts Institute of Technology using Fortran. Fortran was a computer program used in the 50s, mostly for scientific and engineering purposes. In this incident, Fortran was used to make free calls only to accumulate massive phone bills.

Hacking, as most of us know it, is a process of finding vulnerabilities and using these vulnerabilities to obtain unauthorized access to a system to perform malicious activities. Hacking is illegal, and there can be extreme consequences for people who are caught in the act. However, contrary to popular belief, there is a form of legal hacking that is done with permission. It's known as ethical hacking where a professional is hired solely to prevent or fix malicious hacking.

The hero of ethical hacking is Kali Linux. The official website states that Kali Linux is a Linux configuration directed at security testing and penetration. Kali contains tools geared toward security research, as well as reverse engineering.

We are going to learn all about penetration testing, the effect of Kali Linux, and how to use Kali Linux to your advantage to protect your business, as well as personal data.

Offensive Security released Kali Linux in 2013 as a complete rebuild, and it's aimed toward the needs of penetration-testing professionals, and all documentation is tailored to those already familiar with the Linux operating systems in general.

To understand how to use Kali Linux to your advantage, one must begin with the basics of hacking, which includes understanding the difference between ethical and unethical hacking and the types of hackers who exist. Additionally, we must understand how cyberattacks work to know how to stop them.

In this book, we'll be going over all that makes up ethical hacking, as well as cyberattacks and penetration testing.

Chapter 1: What Is Hacking

When you think of hacking, you may imagine something along the lines of someone violently smashing a keyboard, zooming in on things while controlling someone else's computer, and saying things like "I'm in" or "Hack engaged." Or maybe the word hacking makes you think of breaking into someone's Instagram account.

The word "hacking" has preconceived connotations, and most people don't quite grasp the whole concept that goes into the process of hacking. Hackers have a notorious reputation. But there's a side of hacking that most people aren't aware of: ethical hacking. You don't hear about the ethical hacking in the news, but there are people out there with the same job description fighting the malicious hackers daily, and they get the bad rep.

The well-known term "hacking" states it is an attempt to gain unauthorized access to data or a system. So, yes, technically, breaking into your ex's Instagram to read their DM's is a form of hacking, but the term refers to anyone with technical skills in the area of hacking. Humans not only to gain access to accounts but also to stop someone else from gaining unauthorized access.

A History of Hacking

Hacking has been around since as early as the 1960s when, in 1961, a group of MIT students hacked their model trains hacking to modify their functions. That is where the term comes from. So the term hacking is not even directly related to computers! Originally, hacking meant to explore and improve something.

In the 1970s, phone hackers, or "phackers," made their debut when they exploited operational characteristics in phones to gain access to free phone calls, although they were fairly rare. At the time, computer hackers were not yet popular because so few people had personal computers.

This changed in the 1980s when personal computer use gave birth to the first computer hackers. This is no surprise, since when there's a product, there is always someone out there willing to mess with the product to their advantage. Likewise, when there's someone to mess with the product, there is someone to protect it. The birth of computer hacking led to the birth of ethical hacking, as well. The '80s was the decade we first saw hackers breaking into systems to use them for personal gain. This new type of crime naturally called for new legislation. In 1986, the Federal Computer Fraud and Abuse Act was first written. The Act made it a crime for anyone to access a computer used by a financial institution, a government agency, or any organization involved in foreign commerce or communication. This was mainly prompted by the increase in PC use by the general public.

The 1990s was marked by the first high-profile arrests related to hacking. Kevin Mitnick, Kevin Poulsen, Robert Morris, and Vladimir Levin were among the first to get arrested for stealing property software as well as leading digital heists. This was also when the term crackers, meaning those that "crack" into digital encryption codes (e.g. passwords and such), began to be used.

During the late 2000s, the hacking of major companies like eBay, Amazon, and Microsoft often dominated the headlines. This was particularly true when news broke in early 2000 that the International Space Station's system had been breached by 15-year-old Jonathon James.

Modern-day hacking has become more sophisticated than ever. Hacktivists groups, ransomware, and highly classified document releases are a daily problem. In modern times, the ethical hackers are needed more than ever to protect and prevent hack attacks. The information available to everyone makes it all the easier for hack attacks, but it makes protection available as well.

Hacking is not always black and white, and there are different types of hackers and types of hacking. The major types of hackers are divided between ethical, unethical, and somewhere in between.

Ethical Hacker

In the real-world examples, you would call an ethical hacker the firefighter of the group; they put out fires and save innocent lives. They are, more often than not, hired by a government or a law agency to protect data and resolve any harm caused to individuals or businesses. A small business can also hire an ethical hacker to protect the company's data used maliciously or attacked by a malicious hacker.

Unethical Hacker - The Cracker

The unethical hacker, also known as the cracker, is the criminal that gets his information and assets illegally by getting into a device without the owner's knowledge or consent. The intent of this hacking is malicious. This type of hacker causes financial harm, steals confidential data, embezzles funds, disrupts businesses, and spreads incorrect data, among other things.

The Grey Hat

Then there is the hacker who isn't completely ethical or unethical; he's the person that steals to feed the poor. He falls in the gray area between the two other types of hackers. This gray area is where the name grey hat stems from. An example of a grey hat hacker would be a hacker who is hired to protect a particular database and then uses that access to confidential data for personal gain. You may not consider them criminals, but they won't be getting any medals soon. Then you have your "hacktivists," groups such as Anonymous, that use hacking for political and social messages. Finally, there are the "kiddies," or non-skilled people who use already-made tools to gain access to systems. This is when you guess someone's Facebook password because you want to see if they were where they said they were last night.

Types of Hacking

As you can tell, hacking isn't as simple as guessing someone's password and logging into their accounts. There are actually numerous types of hacking that you need to be familiar with.

Phishing

The concept of phishing comes from the everyday activity of fishing. These types of hacks use email or sometimes phone to pose as a legitimate institution to obtain important information that can hurt an individual or a business. Hence, they throw the hook to "fish" for a victim. This usually works by first telling the victim they're a trusted organization, then asking for confidential data.

The first phishing lawsuit was filed in 2004 against a Californian teenager who created a copy of the website called "America Online" where he retrieved credit card information from visitors. One of the first and most popular phishing emails was the infamous "Nigerian Prince" email, which was an email from a "prince" who was stuck and needed your help to get back to his millions. Today, most of us don't fall for the Nigerian Prince scam, but phishing is still alive and problem for millions of internet users. The prevalent phishing -emails are mostly easy to spot. They share a sense of urgency, unusual sender and suspicious hyperlinks. It is when a website is copied and looks like the real thing that things can get complicated. Banking websites can often be targets of phishing because of their extensive access to credit card numbers and sensitive information.

Virus

The purpose of a virus is to corrupt resources on websites. Just like in a human body, the virus can change forms, corrupt the "healthy" programs, and self-propagate. And just like in with us, there are plenty of viruses that can attack your malware.

Topher Crypter Virus is one of the most dangerous types of viruses because of its ability to completely take over the computer, leading to the spread of further viruses. A famous example of a Topher Crypter is the Trojan Virus.

Metamorphic Virus can write, rewrite, and edit its own code. It is the most infectious virus, and it can do massive damage to the computer and data if not detected early.

Polymorphic Virus is similar to a metamorphic virus, but it copies itself; where the metamorphic virus can rewrite its code, the polymorphic just copies its original code with slight modifications.

Macro Virus is written in the same language as software programs such as Microsoft Word or Excel. It starts an automatic sequence of actions every time the application is opened.

Cluster Virus makes it appear as though every program in the system is affected when, in fact, it is only in the one program in the system. It causes the illusion of a cluster and can be removed by figuring out the original "carrier" of the virus.

Tunneling Virus works against antiviruses. It sits in the background and sits under the antivirus. When an antivirus detects virus, the antivirus will try to re-install itself only to install itself as the tunneling viruses.

Stealth Virus uses its mechanism to avoid any detection by antiviruses. The stealth virus will hide in the memory and hide any changes it has made to any files.

Extension Virus will hide in a website or browser extension and create changes through there.

Cookie Theft

Cookies are files stored on your computer used by your browser to save useful information about the websites you visit or any actions you take. Session cookies are temporary and erased once you close your browser. Certain cookies persist in your browser until you yourself erase them or they expire (which could take years). These are called persistent cookies.

Websites use cookies to modify your browsing experience in order to make it tailored to your needs as well as for proper ad placement. Cookie thefts are used by hackers in order to gain access to that information. Cookies are one of the most natural methods of hacking, they can be stolen through public Wi-Fi networks!

UI Redress

UI redress, also called clickjacking, is masking a click in order to gain clicks for a different website. A user might think they are clicking on a straightforward link, but due to clickjacking, they will be redirected to a completely different website. The hacker is "hijacking" clicks. This can get out of control quickly as users will click links that say things such as "win a free vacation," and they will be redirected to a sharing page, causing the clickjacking to spread massively over social media or email.

DNS Spoofing

Domain name server spoofing is an attack in which the domain name is taken over by redirecting the clicks to a fraudulent website. Once there, the users are led to believe they are logging in with their account names and passwords into the original website, but in reality, they are giving away their information to the hacker performing the DNS spoofing. There are a few methods to perform DNS spoofing such as Man in the Middle (where interaction among the server and user is sidetracked) or DNS server compromise (where the server is directly attacked).

The above examples are all types of hacking used by malicious hackers, but ethical hacking also works with them. In order to prevent and "heal" these attacks, the ethical hackers must know how they work, and this is why ethical hackers have to be educated on all the types and methods of hacking used.

Becoming a hacker takes skill, and the ironic part is that both unethical and ethical hackers will use the same education and tools. The only difference is that one will use their "powers" for evil and the other for good (or something in between). It's like a modern-day equivalent of the classic superhero-villain duo Batman and Joker. In order to be a successful ethical hacker, you have to understand malicious hacking as well.

Phases of Ethical Hacking

When it comes to ethical hacking, there are generally five distinct phases:

Reconnaissance - The process of information gathering. In this phase, the hacker gathers relevant information regarding the targeted system. These are things such as detecting services, IP configurations, pc specifications, and password data. The hacker gathers all the information possible (the network, the host, the people involved, etc.).

Scanning - The hacker begins to actively probe the target machine or network for vulnerabilities that can be actively exploited.

Gaining Access - This is one of the essential parts. In this phase, the vulnerability detected during scanning is exploited using various methods—the same methods a malicious hacker might use, but the ethical hacker will use this to know the weak spots of entry. The hacker will try to enter the target system without raising any alarms.

Maintaining Access - Once a hacker has gained access, you want to maintain that access. In malicious hacking, this is used to further gain access to the system so you can exploit and attack, while in ethical hacking, this phase is used to have access to the system you want to protect.

Clearing Tracks - Finally, a malicious hacker wants to cover their tracks so as not to be discovered by security, while an ethical hacker wants to cover their tracks so as not to be discovered by an unethical hacker. The process remains absolutely the same. A hacker can cover his tracks using tunneling protocols or altering log files.

As we can see, hacking is a much different term than the movies like *Hackers* with Angelina Jolie make us believe. While it does look cool to smash a keyboard violently for hours, you have to have an education and intelligence to become a hacker. You also have to have a specific dose of street smarts if you want to work as an ethical hacker because you have to predict the opponent's next move before they make it. It's a mixture of chess and war, an art form of its own. Now that you understand what hacking really is and how ethical hacking differs from malicious hacking, it's time to learn about the types of hackers you can be and how to pick your hacking hat!

Chapter 2: Pick Your Hat

Remember in the *Harry Potter* series when the sorting hat sorts you into which house you're supposed to be in (Slytherin for the bad ones, Gryffindor for the brave ones, etc.). Hacking hats are similar to this, only you're your own sorting hat, and you can switch sides. Let's learn what each means.

To understand the hats hackers metaphorically wear, we must first understand the ethical standards in the hacker communities.

Hacker Ethics

Richard Stallman of the Free Software Foundation, as well as one of the creators of the copyleft concept had the following to say about hacking:

"The hacker ethic refers to the feelings of right and wrong, to the ethical ideas this community of people had—that knowledge should be shared with other people who can benefit from it, and that important resources should be utilized rather than wasted."

The general principles of hacker ethics are:

1. Access to computers must be universal and unlimited

2. All information must be free

3. Encourage decentralization

4. Judge, according to hacks, not according to diplomas, economic stance, race, gender, religion, etc.

5. Create art and beauty with computers

6. Change your life for the better

Black Hat Hacker

The term black hat hacker is derived from old Western movies where the bad guys wore black hats, and the good guys wore—you guessed it—white hats.

The freshest looking color black gets all the bad rap. Villains often wear only black, and then there's death, dark magic and black cats—all associated with dark and evil things. Black hat hackers are thus the ones we hear about in the media the most, the ones using their "powers" for evil.

The black hat hacker is the one that finds security flaws to gain access and uses them for their malicious intents. These can be financial—such as gaining information about credit cards so you can access assets and accounts—or purely informational. Black hat hackers gain access to personal files of celebrities, and they are the ones that will go shopping with your card or even access files from large corporations for larger-scale hacks. Black hat hackers can cause significant damage to an individual or a business, compromising a website or even shutting down security systems.

Black hat hackers range from a kid spreading viruses to major league hackers obtaining credit card passwords. Sometimes, malicious hackers work outside the internet and obtain information through phones by calling and pretending to be a legitimate company. One of the infamous non-computer scams hackers use is pretending to be the IRS or CRS and calling people threatening to take legal action because they haven't paid their taxes. A good rule of thumb to recognize spot this scam is to look for a sense of urgency, like—it has to be paid right here, right now, through your credit card—and the instalment of fear—"if you don't pay this right now you will go to jail!"

Black hat hackers have their conventions, like Comic Con but for hacking. The two famous ones are DefCon and Black Hat. These conventions, however, are often attended by white hat hackers, as well, to learn from the black hats and gain information on anything necessary to know. It's fascinating how close these two worlds have to stay to learn from each other to take each other down.

There are plenty of notorious black hat hackers to choose from, but some stand out even amongst the crowd. Of course, many of the best never got caught, but among those who did get caught are:

Albert Gonzales - He has been accused of the most significant ATM theft in history in the years between 2005 and 2007. When he was arrested, the authorities found $1.6 million cash in his possession as well as $1 million cash around his property, so naturally, he has been sentenced to 20 years in federal prison.

Vladimir Levin - He transferred $10 million from Citibank bank accounts to his own all while hanging out in his apartment. He was discovered when his accomplices tried to withdraw funds from different bank accounts around the world and pointed to him when they were caught. He was arrested and tried for merely three years, and most of the funds have been recovered (apart from $40,000). Media portrayed Levin as a biochemist and a scientist with a Ph.D., but in the later years, it was revealed he was an administrator with not much formal education. Goes to show how sensationalistic it can all get with no actual evidence.

George Hotz - In 2007, at just 17, he was the first person to unlock the iOS security system, and in 2010 he hacked into the Sony system, which resulted in a massive and famous Sony lawsuit. This resulted in the hacking group Anonymous hacking Sony and the most costly security break up to date. He continued to release jailbreak technology up until 2010 when he finally crossed over to the white hat side or more of a gray area.

Johnathan James (aka c0mrade) - At 16 years old, Johnathan became the first person in the United States to go to juvenile prison for cybercrime. At the age of 15, he had broken into the security systems of NASA and the Department of Homeland Defense and stole a software worth over $1 million. He broke into the Defense Threat Reduction Agency and intercepted messages from employees. Johnathan committed suicide at 28, and a past suicide note indicated it may have had something to do with him being implicated in another hacking situation.

Gary McKinnon - McKinnon, from Scotland, hacked into NASA, the US Army, the Air Force, and the Navy systems searching for information about UFOs that he believes the US government is hiding. At one point, a message appeared on all of the computers in the US Army saying "your security system is crap." He has been accused of the largest ever hack of United States government computers, but he was never extradited to the US. The reasons for not doing so was his Asperger's syndrome. Theresa May believed extraditing him would cause more harm than good and that the extradition would be a breach of human rights.

Kevin Mitnick - He started hacking at age 12 by bypassing the punch system in the Los Angeles public bus system. In 1979, at age 17, he gained access to its unauthorized network; following that, he was convicted and sentenced to prison before being given supervised discharge. When he was nearing the end of his probation, he hacked into Pacific Bell computers and fled. He became a fugitive for two and a half years. After a very public pursuit, he was arrested in 1995 on several counts of wire fraud and possession of unauthorized devices. He has been depicted in several movies, books, and comic books, and to this day, he is the most famous black hat hacker.

Hacker Hierarchy

Much like the rest of the world, the hacker world has its own divisions. One of those divisions within the black hat hacker community is based on your hacking skills:

Newbies - They have access to hacker tools but are not very aware of how the programs work.

Cyberpunks - Also known as Green Hat Hackers, they are newbies with more ambition to become coders. They use other tools, but they actively learn to code.

Coders - These are the people who write the programs other hackers use to infiltrate systems.

Cyberterrorists - They infiltrate systems to profit illegally; they are at the top of the hacker food chain.

White Hat Hacker

White hat hackers are what they call the good guys of the hacking industry. They break into systems and do pretty much the same things the black hat hackers do, only the reason behind white hacker hacks is security. They expose vulnerabilities to create higher standards of security before the black hat hackers can take advantage of the system's weaknesses

Often, a former black hat hacker turns white-hat hacker, but you rarely see the opposite. White hat hackers are also known as ethical hackers. In the simplest terms, an ethical hacker tests security networks by pretending to be a malicious hacker to see where the weaknesses are. This means anything from emailing the staff to ask for passwords to testing complicated security systems. This is the reason many black hat hackers switch sides, they get to do the same thing but without the fear of legal prosecution.

Ethical hacking is evident in the US military as well. One of the first instances of ethical hacking was actually conducted by the US Air Force. The idea of ethical hacking didn't come from the Air Force, however. Dan Farmer and Wietse Venema, two programmers, first created the idea of ethical hacking, even if they didn't call it that. Their idea was to raise security on the internet as a whole. Farmer started a software called Computer Oracle and Password System (COPS) designed to identify security weaknesses. Venema designed a Security Administrative Tool for Analyzing Networks (SATAN) that became an accepted method for auditing computer and network security.

Other famous ethical hackers include:

Kevin Mitnick - Yes, the same Kevin Mitnick that was a fugitive is now a famous white hat hacker. After his infamous black hat days, he now works as a consultant and for the FBI. He also acts as a public speaker and teaches classes in universities.

Joanna Rutkowska - She is a cybersecurity researcher focused on Qubes OS. In 2006, she attended a black hat conference and exposed vulnerabilities in Vista Kernel. In 2009, she prevented an attack targeting Intel systems including the Trusted Execution Technology.

Charlie Miller - He is known for exposing vulnerabilities in Apple as well as being the first to locate MacBook Air bug. He spent years working for Uber, and at some point, he even worked for the National Security Agency (NSA). In 2014 he hacked a Jeep Cherokee and managed to control its brakes, steering wheel and acceleration remotely.

Greg Hoglund - He is an author, researcher, and specialist in computer forensics. He contributed to software exploitation and online game hacking and has patented methods for fault injections for white hat hacking purposes. He also founded the popular rootkit.com, a website devoted to the subject of rootkits (collection of computer software designed to enable access that is not otherwise allowed).

Tsutomu Shimomura - This cybersecurity expert and physicist was also involved in tracking down Kevin Mitnick back in his black hat days. Shimomura is the son of a Nobel Prize winner Osamu Shimomura, and he is the founder of Neofocal Systems, company where he served as CEO until 2016. He is also an author of a few books including *Takedown: The Pursuit and Capture of Kevin Mitnick.*

White hat hackers have a harder job and get a lot less credit, but the work they do is a lot more fulfilling and, in the end, legal. While as a black hat hacker some get "cool points," white hat hacking is as equally as interesting. The coolest thing about white hat hacking is all the freedom you get to enjoy because you're not being prosecuted and arrested.

Grey Hat Hackers

Nothing is black and white, and neither are the hacker hats. There is a group of hackers who fall between black and white hackers, called grey hat hackers. So what exactly are grey hat hackers?

They are the hackers who won't always abide by the laws or ethical standards, but they don't have the malicious intents that the black hat hackers do. The term was first coined at a black hat convention DEFCON by a hacker group Lopht, and it was first publicly used in a New York Times interview in 1999.

Lopht described themselves as a group who support the ethical reporting and exposing vulnerabilities but disagree with the full disclosure practices that dominate the white hat communities.

They were also referred to as white hat hackers by day and black hat hackers by night.

It is still not clear as to what a grey hat hacker is because the term is so broad. The general idea is that it is a hacker who will break the law to improve security. You can think of them as the chaotic good of the group.

Some examples of grey hackers are:

Dmitry Sklyarov - In the early 2000s, the Russian citizen, along with his employer, ElcomSoft, caught the attention of the FBI for an alleged violation of the DMCA (Digital Millennium Copyright Act). Sklyarov visited the US to give a presentation called eBooks Security and was arrested on his way back because he had violated the DMCA. The complaint was that Sklyarov and his company illegally obtained copy protection arrangements by Adobe. The US government eventually dropped all charges against him in exchange for his testimony against ElcomSoft.

Julian Assange - Julian Assange, the creator of WikiLeaks, a non-profit that publishes news leaks, is perhaps the clearest example of a grey hat hacker. He began hacking at age 16 and went on to hack NASA, the Pentagon, and Stanford University. He created WikiLeaks in 2006, and it remains an ethical grey area. Some argue that Assange is merely exposing the corruption of elite corporations, while others argue that the work he is doing is illegal and corrupt. One of the most notorious documents released by WikiLeaks is the video of US soldiers shooting 18 civilians from a helicopter in Iraq. Assange has been fleeing the law for years, and he is currently. He is being charged on 17 different counts, and many argue the charges are not valid and a symbol of the end of free journalism.

Loyd Blankenship - Also known as the The Mentor, Blankenship is a well-known writer and hacker. He was a member of different hacker groups including the Legion of Doom. He is the author of the *Hacker Manifesto* and *GURPS Cyberpunk*, which is a cyberpunk roleplaying sourcebook written for Steve Jackson Games. That book landed Blankenship in hot water because it was believed he illegally accessed Bell South and that this would help other groups commit similar hacks.

Guccifer - Guccifer is a Romanian hacker that targeted celebrities. He was the man behind the Hillary Clinton email leak that some argue ultimately caused her downfall in the 2016 presidential elections and got Donald Trump elected. Before Clinton, Guccifer accessed the emails of Romanian starlets. He then moved onto US Secretary of State Colin Powel and George W. Bush.

Anonymous - This is a well-known hacktivist group that has been in the news recently. They are widely known for their attacks against government agencies, institutions, corporations, and the Church of Scientology, but the Anonymous resume list can go on for days. Several people have been arrested for involvement in Anonymous cyberattacks, but to this day, the group still operates.

Hacker hats are all about what you ultimately want to stand for. The idea is the same—penetrate security measures made by individuals and companies. The ethical standpoint behind the hacking decides which hat you want to choose for yourself.

If you are just looking to have some fun testing systems, then stick with the clear-cut white hat hacking. I mean, stick with it in general because it will keep you out of jail.

Chapter 3: How It Works & How to Get Away with It

To completely understand how hacking works would take a lot more than a chapter. Hacking is not exactly a skill that can be taught by reading about it; it is more of a hands-on occupation perfected by time and practice with an inventive mind and a dash of a mischievous spirit.

Hackers work with the computer or program code, which is a set of instructions that work in the background and make up the software. While a lot of hackers do know how to program code, many download and use codes programmed by other people. The main requirement to know is how to work this code and adjust it to their advantage. For malicious hackers, that can be using it to steal passwords, secrets, identities, financial information, or create so much traffic that the targeted website needs to shut down.

Stealing passwords

Passwords are easy to hack because humans are very predictable. We think we are unique until it comes to passwords, but we are very easy to guess. For example, women will often use personal names for passwords—think kids, relatives, old flings—while men will stick to hobbies. The numbers we use most frequently are 1 and 2, and they are most often placed at the end of our password. More often than not, we use one word followed by some number, and if the website insists on including a capital letter, we place it at the beginning of the word and then whine about how this website is so annoying for making us go through all of this.

But how do hackers access our passwords? Well, there are several useful techniques.

The trial and error technique is called the brute force attack, and it is when you try possible combinations of letters and words to try and guess the right password. This can work because, as previously mentioned, we are very predictable when it comes to the type of passwords we use.

Another similar technique is called the dictionary attack; hackers use a file containing all the words that can be found in the dictionary, and the program tries them all. This is why it is often suggested to add numbers to your passwords as words, but this doesn't mean your "sunshine22" password is hackerproof.

A third technique is the rainbow table attack. The passwords in your computer system are hashed (generated into a value or values from a string of text using a mathematical function) in encryption. Whenever a user enters a password, it is compared to an already stored value, and if those match, you are able to enter into the website or application. Since more text can produce the same value, it doesn't matter what letters we input as long as the encryption is the same. Think of it as a door and a key. You enter the doors with the key made for that lock, but if you're skilled at lock picking or a locksmith, you don't need that exact key to enter.

How to protect yourself from password attacks

Use the salt technique. This refers to adding simple random data to the input of a hash function. The process of combining a password with a salt which we then hash is called salting. For example, a password can be "sunshine22" but adding the salt is e34f8 (combining sunshine22 with e34f8) makes your hash-stored, new salted password "sunshine22e34f8." The new salted password is thus hashed into the system and saved into the database. Adding the salt just lowered the probability that the hash value will be found in any pre-calculated table. If you are a website owner, adding salt to each user's password creates a much more complicated and costly operation for hackers. They need to generate a pre-calculated table for each salted password individually, making the process tedious and slow.

Even with the salt technique, determined hackers can pass through the "password salting." Another useful technique is the peppering technique. Just like the salt, pepper is a unique value. Pepper is different than salt because salt is unique for each user, but pepper is for everyone in the database. Pepper is not stored in the database; it's a secret value. Pepper means adding another extra value for storing passwords.

For example, let's say the pepper is the letter R. If the stored password is "sunshine22," the hash stored will be the hashed product of "sunshine22" with the added letter R. When the user logs, in the password they are giving is still "sunshine22," but the added pepper is storing "sunshine22" with the added R. The user has no knowledge that pepper is being used. The website will then cycle through every possible combination of peppers, and by taking upper and lowercase letters, there will be over 50 new combinations. The website will try hashing "sunshine22A," "sunshine22B," and so on until it reaches "sunshine22R." If one of the hashes matches the stored hash, then the user is allowed to log in. The whole point of this is that the pepper is not stored, so if the hacker wants to crack the password with a rainbow table or dictionary attack, it would take them over 50 times longer to crack a single password.

Phishing attacks

The easiest way to get someone's password is to ask them. After all, why bother with all the algorithms and cracking codes when you can just politely ask?

Phishing is often a promise of a prize if you click on a certain link that then takes you to a fake login page where you simply put in your password. The easiest way to defend from this is smart clicking, or not clicking on scammy pop-up ads.

Vacations and iPods are not just given away with a click and "you won't believe what happened next" is a sure sign of a clickbait leading to phishing.

Miracle weight loss pills, enlargement tools, singles waiting to meet you in the area and other promises of luxurious life with just one click are all phishing. Unfortunately, we have to work for money and workout for weight loss.

Back Door Attacks

Imagine you're going to a concert, but you don't have a ticket. You see the line of people all with their purchased tickets waiting to get through security. You see cameras pointing at the front door and a few extra security guards guarding the sides. You don't have a ticket or the money to buy one. Then, you see a little unguarded, dark, hidden alley with no cameras and the back door. The doors that lead to the venue. They are unlocked, and there are no security or cameras around. Would you go through the door? That's the concept behind a back door attack.

How do backdoors even end up on our computers? Well, they can end up there intentionally by the manufacturer; this is built in so they can easily test out the bugs and quickly move in the applications as they are being tested.

The back door can also be built by malware. The classic backdoor malware is the infamous Trojan. Trojan subtly sneaks up on our computer and opens the back door for the people using the malware. The malware can be hidden into anything—a free file converter, a PDF file, a torrent, or anything you are downloading into your computer. Of course, the chances are higher when what you're downloading is a free copy of an otherwise paid product (lesson to be learned here). Trojans have an ability to replicate, and before you know it, your computer is infected with malware that is opening a backdoor for the whole line up to come in to see the show for free.

The back door can be used to infiltrate your system not only for passwords but also for spying, ransomware, and all kinds of other malicious hacking.

How to protect yourself from back door attacks

Choose applications, downloads and plugins carefully; free apps and plugins are a fantastic thing, but YouTube to MP3 converters, torrents of the latest Game of Thrones season, and a copy of Photoshop might not be the best option if you're interested in keeping your passwords safe. Android users should stick to Google Play apps, and Mac users should stick with the Apple store. Track app permissions too and be sure to read, at least a little, before you sign your life away to a third-grade flashlight application.

You can also try:

Monitoring network activity - Use firewalls and track your data usage. Any data usage spike is a sure sign of backdoor activity.

Changing your default passwords - When a website assigns a default password, we may find that we are just too lazy to take the 30 seconds necessary to change it. Just do it. You might not be locking the back door with the latest state-of-the-art security system, but at least you are not keeping them wide open with a neon sign pointing to your password. Freckles might be your puppy, but he can't be a password for everything. A common complaint is, "I will forget it." Write it down. Contrary to popular belief, hackers won't go into your house and search for that piece of paper, but they will go into your computer. Which option seems safer?

Zombie Computers for Distributed Denial of Service (DDoS) attacks

Sounds extremely cool, right? Well, it's not. Basically, a computer becomes a zombie computer when a hacker infiltrates it and controls it to do illegal activities. The best part (for the hacker, not for you) is that you are completely unaware that all this is happening. You will still use it normally, though it might significantly slow down. And then all of a sudden, your computer will begin to send out massive spam emails or social media posts that you have nothing to do with. DDoS attacks are lovely (for the hacker, not for you) because they work on multiple computers at once, and the numbers can go into millions. A million zombie computers are mindlessly wandering around the internet spamming everything in sight, infecting other computers. The version where your computer is infected only to send out spam is the light version. DDoS attacks can also be used for criminal activity, and this is why it is important to prevent them.

How to protect from DDoS attacks

Larger scale businesses require more substantial protection against DDoS attacks, and we will go over that in detail, but even for individuals, half of the protection is prevention.

Understand the warning signs—slowed down computers, spotty connection, or website shutdowns are all signs of a DDoS attack taking place.

What can you do?

Have more bandwidth - This ensures you have enough bandwidth to deal with massive spikes in traffic that can be caused by malicious activity

Use anti-DDoS hardware and software modules - Protect your servers with network and web application firewalls. Hardware vendors can add software protection by monitoring how incomplete connections and specific software modules can be added to the webserver software to provide DDoS protection.

Smart clicking - This should go without saying, but for those in need of hearing it—pop-up ads with a "No, thanks" button are hateful little things. Just exit the website, don't click anything on that ad, especially not the "No, thanks," button or you will instantly activate an annoying download, and now your computer is a zombie.

Man in The Middle

When you're online, your computer does little back-and-forth transactions. You click a link, and your computer lets the servers around the world know you are requesting access to this website.

The servers then receive the message and grant you access to the requested website. This all happens in nanoseconds, and we don't think much about it. That nanosecond moment between your computer and the web server is given a session ID that is unique and private to your computer and the webserver. However, a hacker can hijack this session and pretend to be the computer and as such, gain access to usernames and passwords. He becomes the man in the middle hijacking your sessions for information.

How to protect yourself from the man in the middle

Efficient antivirus and up-to-date software go a long way in preventing hijacking, but there are a couple of other tips that can help you prevent becoming a victim.

Use a virtual private network - A VPN is a private, encrypted network that acts as a private tunnel and severely limits the hacker's access to your information. Express VPN can also mask your location, allowing you to surf the web anonymously wherever you are.

Firewalls and penetration testing tools - Secure your network with active firewalls and penetration testing tools.

Plugins - Use only trusted plugins from credible sources and with good ratings.

Secure your communications - Use two-step verification programs and alerts when someone signs in to your account from a different computer.

Root Access

Root access is an authorization to access any command specific to Unix, Linux, and Linux-like systems. This gives the hacker complete control over the system. Root access is granted with a well-designed rootkit software. A quality designed rootkit software will access everything and hide traces of any presence. This is possible in all Unix-like systems because they are designed with a tree-like structure in which all the units branch off into one root.

The original Unix operating system was designed in a time before the personal computer existed when all the computers were connected to one mainframe computer through very simple terminals. It was necessary to have one large, strong mainframe for separating and protecting files while the users simultaneously used the system.

Hackers obtain root access by gaining privileged access with a rootkit. Access can be granted through passwords; password protection is a significant component in restricting unwanted root access. The rootkit can also be installed automatically through a malicious download. Dealing with rootkit can be difficult and expensive, so it's better to stay protected and keep the possibility of root access attacks to the minimum.

How to protect yourself from root access attacks

Quality antivirus software is one of the standard things recommended in all computers, be it for individuals or businesses. Quality antivirus helps the system hardening making it harder for installation of rootkits.

Principle of least privilege - PoLP is the idea that any program or a user should have only the minimum privileges necessary to perform the programs function. Giving only the bare minimum privilege that a program needs to perform allows for better protection from possible attacks. For example, in a business, a user whose only job is to answer emails should only be given access to the emails. If there is an attack on the user's computer, it can't spread far because the person only has access to email. If a said employee has root access privilege, the attack will spread system-wide.

Disable root login - Servers on most Unix and Linux operating systems come with an option for the root login. Using root login allows for much easier root access, and if you pair it with a weak password, you are walking on a thin line. Disabling the option for root access keeps all the users away from the root login temptation.

Block brute forces - Some programs will block suspicious IP addresses for you. They will detect malicious IP and prevent attacks. While manually detecting is the safest way, it can be a long process; programs that are designed to block malicious IPs can drastically save time and help prevent root access attacks.

The best way to protect yourself from hack attacks is through prevention because the alternative can be lengthy, exhausting, and costly. In the following chapter, we will go into detail about cybersecurity and exactly how you can prevent all the possible attacks on your system.

Chapter 4: Cybersecurity

The internet is a vast place, and most people are not experts on protecting the information about them that is available. It's no surprise that there are people out there who take advantage of others' ignorance. But there are ways to protect yourself from those kinds of attacks, and that's where cybersecurity comes in.

What Is Cybersecurity?

By the time you finish reading this sentence, over 300 million people will have clicked on a single link. You are part of a universe that generates information every millisecond. We do everything from home—buy, sell, eat, drink, fight, tweet, click, and share. We don't need to go to the movies to see a movie or go to the stores to shop. Information exchanges happen online every time you connect to Wi-Fi, publish content, buy something online, like a post on social media, click a link, send an email...you get the gist. We produce much more information than we can grasp, so we underestimate the quantity and value of protecting it.

Cybersecurity is the protection of hardware, software, and data from cyberattacks. Cybersecurity ensures data confidentiality, availability, and integrity. A successful and secure system has multiple layers of protection spread across the networks, computers, data, and programs. For cybersecurity to be effective, all the people involved in different components must complement each other. It is always better to prevent cyberattacks then deal with the consequences of one.

Cyberattacks hit businesses every day. The latest statistics show that hackers now focus more on quieter attacks, but they are increased by over 50%.

During 2018, 1% of websites were considered victims of cyberattacks. Thinking about 1% of all websites that exist, that adds up to over 17 million websites that are always under attack. Cyberattacks cost an average of $11 million per year, so cybersecurity is a crucial aspect of saving your business much money.

That's where the most prominent problem occurs. Small business owners and individuals don't grasp the potential threat to their data because they don't see the value they bring to a hacker attacking. The value is in the lack of security.

Many small businesses with no security are more accessible to penetrate than one large corporation. Corporations invest in cybersecurity; small business owners and individuals do not. They use things like the cloud. Their data migrate with them to the cloud allowing criminals to shift and adapt. The lack of security on their part is crucial to these statistics. The most definite form of on-going attacks remains ransomware; it is so common-place that it is barely even mentioned in the media. Ransomware infects a website by blocking access to their data until a business or an individual transfer a certain amount of money. Hackers hold your data hostage, and it's always about the money.

Cybersecurity is not complicated, it is complex. However, it is also very important to understand. Implementing just the top four cybersecurity strategies diminishes attacks by over 70%. Here are some of the techniques:

Application whitelisting - allowing only approved programs to run

Applications security patching - enforcing security patches (fixes) promptly for applications

Operating systems security patching - enforcing security patches (fixes) promptly for the whole system

Limiting administrative privileges - allowing only trusted individuals to manage and monitor computer systems

Cybersecurity Benefits

There's a variety of benefits cybersecurity can bring to you or your business, and some aren't as obvious as you may think.

Prevents ransomware - Every 10 seconds, someone becomes a victim of ransomware. If you don't know what is happening in your network, an attacker probably found a way to get into it.

Prevents adware - Adware fills your computer with ads and allows the attacker to get into your network.

Prevents spyware - The attacker can spy on your activity and use that information to learn about your computer and network vulnerabilities

Improves your search engine rankings - SEO is the key in the modern digital market. Small businesses looking to rank up on search engines have to be educated in SEO if they want to advance financially. HTTPS (HyperText Transfer Protocol Secure), or the encryption of username, passwords, and information, is one of the critical SEO ranking factors.

Prevents financial loss and saves your startup - More than half of small business go down after a cyberattack. The downtime required to fix the damage prevents any new business, and the data breach causes you to lose the trust of your current customers. Stable businesses can find a way to recover from this, but startups rarely make it out alive.

Cybersecurity Fundamentals

In order to fully understand cybersecurity, there are a few terms you need to be familiar with. They are listed below.

Authentication is verifying the source of any received information. This comes down to a few crucial factors—something you know, have, or you are.

Something you know - Your pin or a piece of information other users don't know like the street you grew up on or your favorite teacher.

Something you have - A badge, token or a key.

Something you are - Fingerprint authorization or a voiceprint.

Whatever method you're using, the basic idea is to use a challenge that a person must answer. Multifactor authentication is when a system requires more than one factor of authentication. Authentication applies to validate the source of a message, but they rely on cryptographic signatures, or a hash of a message generated with a secret key.

Authorization focuses on diagnosing what the user has permission to do. After a user is authenticated, the system needs to determine what privileges they hold. An online banking app authenticates its user by a password, pin code, or a fingerprint. Once they are in, the app authorizes what accounts they have access too. The app determines which actions this user can perform based on their authorization, such as transfers or viewing balances.

Nonrepudiation is the contract between a user and the sender of data, so no parties can deny the data processing in the future. In a cyber world, there can be no signatures and notaries, but a type of contract is necessary for proper cybersecurity. Secure systems rely on asymmetric cryptography. Symmetric key systems use one key encrypt and decrypt data; asymmetric key systems use a pair—one for signing data and the other for verifying it.

Confidentiality is a term most people are familiar with. It means insurance that data is not exposed to unapproved people, methods, or machines. Assurance of confidentiality can be broken down into three significant steps.

First, the information must have capable protections from unauthorized users accessing it. Second, there must be a limit on the information released even to those users who are authorized. Third, it must be used to verify all identities.

Now, you ask, how do I protect the information I don't want taken? Protect the information by storing it into a private location on a private network. Using a VPN and encrypting messages to restrict viewing are both crucial factors in maintaining confidentiality. Stay alert in the physical world as well. Shoulder surfing, the act of looking over a person's shoulder, is a high-risk threat many people don't take seriously. Breaching confidentiality can cause your business significant lawsuits and end up costing you a tremendous amount of money.

Integrity is ensuring that the stored data is accurate and contains no false or misrepresented information or unauthorized modifications. This principle prevents those without authorization from modifying data. Weak software can lead to accidental losses in data integrity and open the system to unauthorized modifications. Disrupting the identity of data can have serious consequences. Imagine an attacker disrupting an online transfer. They can adjust and hijack a message from the user to the receiver and modify the information to their benefit, resulting in the funds ending up on a different account.

Availability is access to the users. Without access to the users, the systems provide no value. Attacks such as DoS (denial of service) show how vital availability is. One form of DoS is resource exhaustion. The attacker overflows the system with requests, so the system no longer responds to legitimate requests. Another form of DoS is network flooding where the attacker sends so much traffic the system can no longer respond to any good traffic.

A good way to prevent yourself from getting a virus, and therefore giving someone unintended access to your computer is using a firewall.

Firewalls

The word firewall is thrown around the internet, but so many people don't know how they work or what they mean. The growth of the internet made them vital to protecting computers. The primary use for a firewall is simple: Keep the bad guys out.

Before starting to understand firewalls, the critical concept to understand is data packets. When we want to download a file of, for example, 1GB, we won't receive the entire 1GB of data at once.

We receive small data packets of 5 MB per second. Some of these packets contain information like which computer is sending the data and which computer is receiving it. The part of the actual data combined with sender-receiver information forms a data packet or IP packet aka payload.

There are three generations of firewalls:

Packet Filters act by inspecting the "packets" that transfer between computers. When you are downloading a file from the internet, this firewall checks the sender and receiver's IP address and the port number, which are the digits in the IP address separated by a colon. The rules are written in a list called an access control list. The firewall checks the rules set and allows or denies the data package to pass to the computer. The packet filtering firewall is present in the routers. They are the cheapest and quickest option for firewalls. The packet filter firewalls do not check the payload section of the data packet, so a hacker could send malicious data hidden in the payload section. Packet filtering firewall is best used in a very low-risk environment.

Application/Proxy Firewall is best explained with a real-life example. Let's say your manager sends you to the store to buy some printing paper. You buy printing paper and bring it back to the manager. You have performed a task your manager wanted you to do, but the sales associate is unaware of who wanted the printing paper. Replace the sales associate with the internet, your manager with your computer, and yourself with a proxy firewall. Proxy firewalls don't let the internet know which computer wants to visit the requested website. Proxy firewalls hide us from attackers online. Application firewalls check the payload of the received data package, so they are generally much slower than packet filters.

Hybrid Firewall combines the packet filter firewall and application firewall providing the best security and speed. Hybrid firewall is best used for high-risk environments such as banks or hospitals.

Virtualization

Today's computers have strong processing power, fast CPU speeds, fast and inexpensive RAM, and storage capacity; that power is under-utilized when the hardware and processing power is not being used.

Virtualization helps solve the problem of underutilized resources by creating the layer between the hardware users and the components.

Your computer grants different software different privileges. The operating system has more privileges than regular programs; for example, it is able to access your memory or your CPU for protection against malicious attacks. A virtualization system is allowed to run as a regular program without the privileged access. In the past, the virtualization resulted in high cost; in the mid-

2000s, AMD and Intel started making processors that natively supported virtual machines. These processors meant that the system wouldn't have to spend time translating instructions.

Virtual machines are useful in testing new software or testing a website because you can delete the virtual machine without losing any of the critical data. If you want to test Windows applications on your Mac, you can do so safely with virtualization because your virtual machine won't touch your core. Virtualization is also extremely effective against viruses as the virus doesn't affect your processor, and you can get rid of your virtual machine. VM's are an easy way to back up relevant data that you can't lose. A majority of available VM software can take snapshots of the whole virtual system. Running multiple virtual machines at once can put processing power to better use.

Memory Forensics

Memory forensics is finding and extracting forensic artifacts from a computer's physical memory. On any given computer, everything you do converts to memory at some point. We use memory forensics to ascertain facts such as:

- Processes running

- Open ports

- Users logged into the system and their location

- Files that are open in the system and by whom

Random-access memory (RAM) encloses essential information about the current state of the computer. By capturing the full copy of RAM on a different computer, it is possible to reconstruct the state of the original system.

Passive Analysis

The passive analysis is the hands-off approach to behavioral malicious code investigation. It is necessary to have a computer to infect and a way to catch the state of the infected computer. Finally, you can restore it to the original system. Passive analysis systems have three cycles:

First, somebody installs the system and necessary applications on a computer, recording the state of the computer. The recorded data includes any features of the system that malicious code might change.

Second, the malicious code in question is executed on the system for some time. The amount of time depends on how quickly the analysis must be performed. Two- to three-minute runtimes are common, as this is usually a sufficient amount of time for the malicious code to complete its initial installation. After the malicious code infects the system, it must be shut down before an external system analyzes its disk and memory to record the new "infected" state. An external computer may be used to record the infected system's state to avoid any interference from the malicious code. Malicious code often hides files and processes from the user using rootkits, but an external system (such as a virtual machine host or a system working from a copy of the infected disk) is not susceptible to this interference. During the analysis stage, the external system compares the infected state to the clean state already recorded. Standard analysis features include the following.

- File system

- Windows Registry content

- Running processes

- Listening ports

- Memory contents

Active analysis

Active analysis programs install software that's soon to be infected. AMAs monitor malicious code and keep a log of its activity. This process shows which malicious code made changes to the system during the infection, and it records which process took each action. The active approach injects packets into systems or sends them to servers and applications.

The Importance of Cybersecurity

We no longer question if the information we have available is true. This often makes us vulnerable to misinformation, and sometimes, this can put our whole lives at risk.

The danger in living online is that we put so much of ourselves out there. If a malicious hacker gets ahold of our information, they can change our image, modify the truth, and change our lives forever. Organizations try their best to control this, but individuals don't do the same. We have to adjust our online behaviors and take security seriously so that we maintain control of our lives online.

We have to leverage cybersecurity to create better lives. The average person deals and conducts transactions online without fully understanding how and what they're doing.

Cybersecurity is like the brakes on a car. It doesn't stop you from where you're going; it allows you to control the way there.

Chapter 5: Getting To Grips With Kali Linux

Kali Linux is a Linux distro made primarily with white hat hacking in mind. It's been designed entirely for the sake of digital forensics and penetration testing.

Kali Linux comes with several desktop environments and kernel architectures. A kernel is the core of an operating system, or the central part of an operating system.

Kernels have four major categories:

Monolithic kernels - A monolithic kernel is an operating system architecture where the entire operating system is working in kernel space and is alone in supervisor mode. The monolithic module differs from other operating system architectures. The advantage of using a monolithic kernel is that it provides CPU scheduling, memory and file management, and other operating system functions through system calls.

Microkernels - The philosophy behind microkernels is that you want to keep the kernel as small and straightforward as possible. It's much harder to write kernel code, and there can be many bugs in it.

Exokernels - Exo is even smaller than micro. You're allowing each application to pick its libraries.

Hybrid - A hybrid is formed by the two operating systems (the monolithic and microkernel).

What this means is that you can run Kali on a variety of environments.

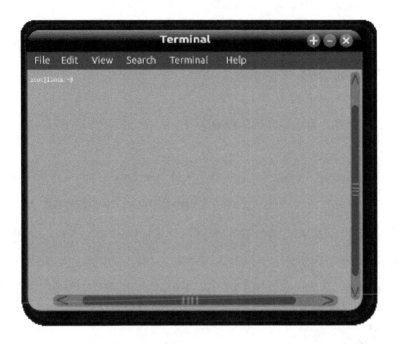

Desktop Environments

The big difference in Windows and Unix/Linux systems is that they are modular in design. Unix, the father of Linux, operates based on small interactive programs that are chained together to perform more substantial tasks.

The GPU (graphics processing unit) toolset is a large component set that helps the kernel interact with the hardware. The GUI (graphical user interface) can be changed or completely removed from the operating system without any effect on the working parts. Linux can operate as anything from a smartwatch to a massive hacking device. GUI includes folders, wallpapers, icons, toolbars, and interfaces for applications.

In Kali, desktop environment interacts with a Windowing System that runs directly on top of the hardware.

Enlightenment (E17) desktop

Enlightenment is one of the original desktops still in existence; it was released in 1997. It was redeveloped as a rewrite in 2012, and since then, it has been maintained by Samsung. Enlightenment is the most used Linux desktop because it appears on every TV sold in the previous years. It's lightweight, you can configure it in many ways, and it can be visually stunning.

Enlightenment 17 desktop issues

- Takes a long time to configure due to so many possible modifications.

- Almost all security measures are categorized together under the "other menu."

- Enlightenment is currently on version E22, but Kali works best with E17.

Gnome desktop

Most users can grasp the Gnome desktop, even those with little experience with Linux. You only see the top bar with everything else being hidden until you need it.

The dash contains three icons by default, and the rest is added according to the frequency of use. New desktops are created automatically, so there's always one empty desktop available when needed.

Gnome 3 desktop issues

- Apps open one at a time. You switch to the activities screen each time.

- There are no icons on the desktop. For some users, this is a positive, but some consider this a deal-breaker.

KDE desktop

The KDE desktop is one of the fastest and has features that can transform the user experience. Hovering the mouse over a minimized task opens a pop-up preview, making the cluttered desktop workspace easy to maneuver.

KDE has applications such as Kontact for personal information management, digiKam for image management, and Amarok for music. These programs are helpful for organization and easy to use once you learn how.

KDE issues

- The only way to change the background panel is to change the general desktop theme.

- Menu and option organization is cluttered and not alphabetically organized, making it a prolonged task to search for an application a user needs.

LXDE desktop

LXDE is a lightweight desktop and great for older computers and slower hardware. It is very automatic for users who previously used Windows and very easy to install.

LXDE issues

- Desktop appearance. The computer looks like an old machine, so it's not the best choice for those looking for visual satisfaction. The desktop also lacks the unified settings window.

MATE desktop

MATE desktop is highly configurable because it comes with an option to configure it like Windows, Mac, or Gnome. You don't have to learn from scratch.

It works great on old computers because it doesn't have a lot of requirements.

MATE issues

- Not a very good software center.

- Not for those who want the latest and fastest desktops available.

Xfce desktop

Xfce is fast, lightweight, and user-friendly. Users report a fantastic balance between simplicity and usability. It works like the classic Windows and Gnome desktop, so it is easy to learn and adjust. XFCE is designed for productivity; it loads applications fast while conserving resources. It is the best choice for those new to Linux.

Xfce issues

- Visually unappealing. It looks a bit dated and lacks modern effects.

- It is missing some basic functionality like a file-archiver, so you have to find alternatives.

Installing Kali Linux on A Virtual Box

Once you've chosen your desktop environment, it's time to learn how to set up and configure your versions of the platform. Kali Linux has various common and uncommon uses, ranging from penetration testing to personal use.

Kali Linux is one of the most exceptional security packages for an ethical hacker. Kali Linux can be installed in the hardware or as a virtual machine, live CD or a USB.

Download and Install the Virtual Box

Running the program on a virtual box is a safe way to test something if you are unsure. You can go here (https://www.virtualbox.org/wiki/Downloads) to download your virtual box. Once you've installed the virtual box, you can go ahead and install Kali Linux. (htpps://www.kali.org/downloads/

Open your virtual box and click "new," choose Kali Linux, and open. Once the screenshot pops up, click the create button. The username for Kali Linux is "root," and the password is "toor."

Updating

It's crucial to update Kali Linux frequently. To do so, go to the application terminal and type in *apt-get update*, and to upgrade the tools, type in *apt-get upgrade.*

To upgrade to a newer version type in *apt-get distupgrade.*

Installing Kali Linux on an Encrypted USB Drive

A warning before you begin: You should use these tools only on systems you have written authorization to test or systems that are your own. Any use of these instructions on a machine you do not have the authorization to test is illegal under various laws. You will go to jail. Get a copy of the testing waiver from your company that allows testing the client's network and systems. This document contains the dates and times of testing and the IP addresses and networks to be tested. Do not test without this.

Secure network environments with IT departments present certain challenges to security engineers. The companies have lists of approved applications, and security tools are miscategorized as malicious hacking tools or malware packages. Companies also have rules against using any operating system that isn't Microsoft Windows already installed on the hardware.

There are very few penetration testing tools written for Windows. The most reliable option is a USB stored with Kali Linux, that is both bootable and encrypted. On Kali's install screen, there is an option to install Kali to a USB drive with something called persistence.

Persistence means the ability to install a USB drive and save files, but the USB is not encrypted. The USB is not compromised, and if lost, the data is still safe. The recommended size of the USB is 64 GB. You can use a smaller one, but there is a lot of data, so the 64 GB proves to be the safest option. You also need a copy of Kali on a DVD and a computer with a DVD player.

Insert the USB before powering the machine, so the machine sees the USB on boot, and the installer sees it during the install. Insert your DVD.

Next, power up the machine and in the Kali screen, pick the graphical install option or pick the install command on line six.

Screens for setting the country, language, and keyboard appear. After configuring, you see a window to supply a hostname. Give it a new name, not the default one.

You are then asked for a domain name. Give it a real domain name you or your company control. In the next window, provide a root password. Please choose a strong password because after a few tests your entire network will be on this device. Finally, choose a time zone and location.

Setting up the drive

The next window asks to select the type of partitioning. Pick guided and use the option for the entire disk and set up encrypted LVM. This fully encrypts the entire drive as opposed to just home/directory. Pick a disk to install the Kali Linux drive on to. Pick the USB disk NOT your local drive because picking local drive wipes out the entire operating system.

In the next window, choose the default. Save the partitioning information and click continue. All data is now on the disk; you can click yes to this and continue. The process is starting; it takes a while, so you can make some plans in the meantime.

In the next window, create a paraphrase. Use something easy to remember but challenging for a malicious hacker like a quote or a song lyric. Click finish partitioning and then continue. Now the partitioning process starts—another good time to meet some friends. When the question "do you want to use a Network Mirror" pops up, say yes. Your process is finally finished, and you can reboot the system. Remove the install disk before rebooting!

Booting your installation of Kali

Insert the USB into the machine and power it up. When a menu of available drives to boot from pops up, pick the USB drive and continue. The system now asks for the passphrase, which is that lyric or quote you put in earlier. Now the booting process begins. After the booting process is finished, the login screen appears. Its appearance might vary depending on the computer desktop you have installed.

Log in and continue set up. Check that everything is up to date as there might be a few necessary updates.

In the Enlightenment 17 desktop:

Log into the Terminal emulator screen with your root credentials, and then type startx to open the GUI.

In the Gnome desktop:

Click the applications menu bar in the upper left-hand corner.

Go to Applications | Usual applications | System tools | Terminal.

In the same applications menu, go to *Applications | Favorites | Terminal.*

-metal install (as opposed to a virtual machine installation), you can hit *Alt + F2* to open a run dialogue, then type gnome-terminal.

Any of these should bring up the terminal or command line window. Type the following:

root@kalibook :~# apt-get update. This refreshes the update list and checks for new updates. Next, run: *root@kalibook :~# apt-get -y upgrade.* This runs the upgrade process as the -y automatically answers yes to the upgrade. The system runs upgrade of all applications. Reboot if necessary.

Whether you're installing Kali Linux directly to your computer or a laptop, it's essential to do a few things after setting it up to make sure it's secure and directly available. Every installation of Kali Linux isn't the same because they come from different package types. All the tools must be appropriately updated. It can be challenging to go back and track what needs updating, so follow these steps to have all the proper tools.

Install git

The first thing you want to do is install git because it allows you to download samples of code. To install git in your Kali Linux type: *apt install git.* Shortly after, you should be able to go to a git repository and install. To install go to your git repository, click "clone or download," copy and paste after typing get a clone, and all the work in your git repository is now cloned locally to your computer.

Set up bash aliases

Now that you've installed git, the next thing you need to do is to configure any bash aliases for any applications that you'll frequently be using. To update bash aliases in Kali Linux type *nano-/.bash_aliases*, and when you press enter this should open a list of aliases. To create an alias, try this example: Type *alias hackwifi= 'besside-ng wlan o'* which is a standard Wi-Fi hacking command that a hacker might use using the internal wireless adapter to start a wireless attack. Save the modified buffer, press enter, and open a new terminal window to test it out. Type *hackwifi* and press enter.

Set up a new low privileged user

Set up a low privileged user to make sure you are not continually logging in as root and thus making it easier for an attacker to take over the system. This is critical because if we are running a piece of software that is running as root, it can take over our computer without running any other intervention. Type *adduser* followed by the name of the user account that we want to add. After pressing enter, it will edit your directory and prompt for a password twice, followed by some more questions. Once you've added that information and certified that it's correct, the user is added to your system. Next, you can go ahead and add this user to the sudo-users group by typing *usermod-aG sudo accountnamenotroot.* This gives your new account sudo user permission so if you need to use root you can by typing in the password.

Install a terminal multiplexer

The terminal multiplexer allows your computer to run multiple scripts all within the same window. Typically, you have to go between different terminal windows to run a script that enables or requires things to run in multiple tabs, but in this case, you can do all that within one terminal window. Just type *apt install tilix.* Once it is done installing, you can run it just by typing *tilix.* You can test it by opening a new window; you see the options for adding the new windows allowing you to run multiple windows at once.

Install hacking tools

Depending on your version of Kali Linux, this step requires you to download and install any packages that might not have been included. If you're using a smaller version of Kali Linux, you can install tools related to your goal without needing to install them one by one. To check this out go to <u>this link</u> (https://tools.kali.org/kali-metapackages) where you can find more information about kali meta-packages.

There are wireless tools, software-defined radio toolkit, forensics tools, and many more.

Install the latest version of Tor

Tor is an important tool for privacy and censorship that's well known by most hackers, but because of this, it is also a target for anyone developing exploits. You have to have your Tor updated. It's best to get it directly from the source and add the source type in the following command: *echo 'deb https://deb.torproject.org/torproject.org stretch main deb-src https://deb.torproject.org/torproject.org stretch main' > /etc/apt/sources.list.d/tor.list*

Then continue to download the Tor Package Signing Key (https://www.torproject.org/docs/debian.html.en) to verify the package that you are receiving. Copy the command: *wget-O- https://deb.torproject.org/torproject.org/A3C4F0F979CAA22 CDBA8F512EE8CBC9E886DDD89.asc | sudo apt-key add -*

Paste it into the terminal window. Once this is installed, you can go back and find the correct way to update this from now on, after running an apt update to run *apt-get install tor deb.torproject.org-keyring*.

Config file sharing with Syncthing

Setting up Syncthing will allow us to easily sync files between our computer or a virtual installation and the computers we use daily.

This can be useful if you discover something or want to transfer data you found in your Kali installation to another computer because otherwise, you are relying on a USB stick or some other physical means of transfer.

Go to your Kali terminal window and put in the command as follows: *apt-get update && apt-get install apt-transport-https -V*

This downloads and installs the primary requirement for Syncthing. Next, import the PGP keys by typing the following: *curl -s https://syncthing.net/release-key.txt | sudo apt-key add -*

PGP keys ensure that we are not downloading the modified version of the program or that our communications are being intercepted. Next, add the Syncthing to your repository by using the echo command: *echo 'deb https://apt.syncthing.net/ syncthing stable' >> /etc/apt/sources.list*

Adding the Syncthing to your repository means you should be able to apt getupdate and see it appear as something that you can install. Finally, type in one more command: *atp install syncthing*

Now that this is downloaded you can go ahead and type syncthing and run it for the first time.

Install code editor

Atom is a free, customizable text editor so you can start editing code on the fly. Atom includes many modules that enable code sharing in real-time, code autocompletion, and the ability to install packages.

You first need to make sure to have all the requirements. To install the required dependencies, copy the following command: *apt-get install gvfs gvfs-common gvfs-daemons gvfs-libs gconf-service gconf2 gconf2-common gvfs-bin psmisc*

This installs everything you need to run Atom. You can download tatom from their website here (https://atom.io/download/deb). Finally, use dpgk with the (-i) argument: *dpkg -i ~/Downloads/atom-amd64.deb*

When this is done, you can find Atom in your applications menu.

Clone Rubber Ducky encoder

Rubber Ducky encoder allows you to write and encode human interface device attacks for the USB rubber ducky.

First, download the tool that's used to flash the rubber ducky. Go to your terminal window and input: *git clone https://github.com/hak5darren/USB-Rubber-Ducky*

Type in *cd USB-Rubber Ducky# ls* to see the available different files. Change into the USB-Rubber-Ducky/Encoder/ directory and use the java command to start encoding ducky payloads without third-party websites.

You can do this with: cd USB-Rubber-Ducky/Encoder/ and java -jar encoder.jar -i input_payload.txt -o inject.bin

Change default password and SSH keys

The final thing on the list is to setup SSH Keys and setup default passwords because either one can represent a severe security vulnerability. The default password is the same for every Kali Linux Installation: Toor. Default password makes it very easy to automate attacks, and the default SSH keys can allow an attacker to intercept your communications.

To change your SSH keys type *cd/etc/ssh/* in your Kali Linux terminal window. This allows you to go ahead and type *dpkg-reconfigure openssh-server*. This resets your SSH keys from the default ones. This is a crucial step to making sure that your communications are secure. Next, type *passwd root*; this lets you change the default password for the root account. Type in your new password.

Once you follow these steps on your Kali Linux installation, it should be set up, secure, and able to use all the great tools that Kali has to offer.

Chapter 6: Penetration Tests

Penetration testing, PT, pen testing, or ethical hacking is a legal and authorized attempt to locate and successfully exploit computer systems for the purpose of making them secure. Hackers exploit the vulnerabilities of a system using code. To do so they can use various tools.

Penetration testing is a white hat hacker action which means they have permission, authorization, and the necessary paperwork. Without permission and authorization, this becomes a black hat hacker action.

Penetration testing is essential for several reasons:

- Identifies a simulation environment and how a malicious hacker may attack the system through the white-hat attack.

- Helps to find weak spots where an intruder can attack to gain unauthorized access to the machine's features and data.

- Offers supports to avoid black hat attacks and protects the original data.

- Helps estimate the extent of the attack on a business (or even an individual).

- Provides evidence as to why it is essential to increase investments in the security aspect of technology and data protection.

- Categorizes the vulnerabilities in your system by suggesting where the weakest points are.

- Keeps your business activities updated and complies with the laws and regulations.

Additionally, a breach of business security can cause damage worth millions of dollars. This is due to lost time—time that could be spent working with clients and controlling the damage. Penetration testing protects your organization from these damages by making sure these attacks don't happen in the first place.

Even a single customer's data breach may cause big financial damage as well as reputation damage. Penetration tests keep the data secure and your company's reputation solid.

Using BackTract

BackTrack Penetration for penetration testing is a predecessor to Kali Linux, and it was a standard package of tools used to expedite penetration testing. Offensive Security released BackTrack to provide a variety of tools for the defense geared toward auditors, administrators, and security professionals interested in improving network security. Naturally, the unauthorized penetration hackers got a hold of the same tools. In BackTrack, the penetration testing tools were in the /pentest directory and subfolders /web or /database.

Kali Linux suppressed BackTrack and is now using a distinct platform structure based on the old Debian GNU/Linux operating system. Instead of navigating through the /pentest tree, you can locate a tool from anywhere on the system because applications are in the system path.

Kali has a few other advantages, such as:

- Multiple desktop environments supported in different languages.

- Tools are synchronized at least three times a day, making it easier to apply security fixes and update as necessary.

- Support for ISO customizations where users can build customized versions of Kali.

- ARMEL and ARMHF support allow Kali installation on a variety of machines.

- A choice of over 300 defensive and penetration tools that provide extensive wireless support and kernel patches to allow the packet injection sometimes required by specific wireless attacks.

Penetration testing is a specialty that needs to be conducted periodically to ensure the security of the system. In addition to regular performance, penetration testing should be done every time a security system discovers new threats by attackers. It is advisable to test when you add a new network infrastructure or when you update your system or install new software. To be safe, perform a penetration test when you relocate your office or set up a new end-user program/policy.

Methodologies for Penetration Testing

Testers and attackers alike use informal or open-source methodology. Methodology means recognizing the parts that can be performed automatically so the testers (and attackers) can focus on updated techniques to explore vulnerabilities. The results allow the testers (or attackers) to compare over time and to compare one tester's final results with the others. These results are also a way to see how much security changes over time.

The defined methodology allows costs management because it is predictable. Companies are aware of staff and time necessary to perform pen-testing, so there are no unforeseen costs. Clients can pre-approve methodologies, so the tester is protected against any liability in case of damage to data or networks.

Formal methodologies include the following examples:

Open Source Security Testing Methodology Manual (OSSTMM)

With this, a verified and detected risk has to be categorized. OSSTMM refers to these limitations as the inability of protection mechanisms to work correctly. The purpose of the OSSTMM is to supply a scientific methodology for the specific characterization of operational security and adaption for penetration tests, security, and ethical hacking.

Open Web Application Security Project (OWASP)

This is focused on the 10 most prevalent vulnerabilities in web-based applications. These vulnerabilities are injection flaws, such as SQL, QS, and LDAP; weak authentication and session administration; cross-site scripting (XSS); unstable direct object reference; safety misconfiguration; delicate data exposure; absent function level access control; cross-site request forgery (CSRF); using components with known vulnerabilities; and unvalidated redirects and forward.

Penetration Testing Execution Standard (PTES)

This is a complete methodology that accurately reflects on the activities of a potential hack if actively maintained. The procedure is made of seven sections that the ethical hacker follows. The methodology starts with the pre-engagement interactions, then moves to intelligence gathering, possible threats, vulnerability exposure and exploitation, post-exploitation, and finishes with a detailed report for the client.

The "Kill Chain"

Mike Cloppert, the director of global CTI, coined the concept and the term "attacker kill chain." These are the steps taken by a malicious hacker when they are attacking a network. While it has a method, the "kill chain" sometimes proceeds in a linear flow and sometimes in a parallel flow.

The phases of a kill chain are as follows:

Reconnaissance

The reconnaissance phase is when the attackers are learning everything they possibly can about the target. Not only do they learn about the business and networks, but they gather information about the key players, their lives, friends, families, and anything useful they can find about them. Over 50 percent of the penetration test or an attack is spent conducting reconnaissance!

Generally, there are two types of reconnaissance:

Passive reconnaissance – This is where the hacker reviews the publicly available website(s), assesses social media and other online sources, and attempts to determine the weaknesses of the target. Hackers generate a list of past and current employee names, family members names, and general hobbies to use as a base to try to guess passwords. This type of reconnaissance is dangerous because it is complicated, some say even impossible, to see the difference in the behavior of a user like me and you and a malicious hacker.

Active reconnaissance - The target can detect active reconnaissance, but it can be difficult to distinguish from regular backgrounds. Activities occurring during active reconnaissance are technical, and they include the scanning of potential ports, weaknesses, and target bases.

Delivery

Delivery is the development of the weapon that is used to complete the attack. The exact weapon chosen depends on the attacker's intent and the route of delivery (through the network, wireless, or a website).

The exploit/compromise phase

The exploit phase is the point when an exploit is successfully applied, and the attacker reaches the objective of the attack.

The compromise can occur in a single phase (a vulnerability exploited using a buffer overflow) or a multiphase (an attacker physically accessed premises to steal an object such as a USB).

Multiphase attacks occur more often when an attacker focuses on the enterprise of choice.

Post-exploit

The post exploit action of the objective is sometimes incorrectly referred to as the "exfiltration phase" because of the belief that the attacks are only trying to steal sensitive data such as passwords, financial information, or authorized access. Sometimes an attacker has a different goal, such as to cause problems in a competitor's network and redirect customers to their website.

One of the most common exploit activities is when the attackers try to gain access privileges to the essential level, also known as vertical escalation, and to hack as many accounts as possible, also known as horizontal escalation.

There is value in accessing a system, and the higher the persistent access, the higher the value to the hacker. This part of the kill chain is the simplest to detect. Kill chains are models of an attacker's behavior, but they don't always follow the exact route as a lot of the attack depends on the defense. However, it ensures a strategy to follow when creating a security system and a way to focus on how an attacker might approach the system or a network.

The Stages of Penetration Testing

Penetration testing, as a process, is made up of 4 fundamental stages, each of which is equally important. The stages are:

1. *Planning and reconnaissance*

Active reconnaissance is when a hacker is defining the goals of a penetration test, including which system to address and the methods best suited for the task. Professional security needs to gather all intelligence (domain names, mail server, network names) to understand how a target works and its vulnerabilities. Reconnaissance information is available anywhere on the internet or other public sources and is also known as OSINT (open-source intelligence). The amount of available information for everyone to access is unnerving and plentiful. OSINT collection and analysis are lengthy and complicated, so we will just go through the basics.

The collected information depends on the goal of the attack or defense.

For financial information, the hacker first needs the personal information of relevant employees (CFO, CEO, and so forth), followed by their passwords and usernames and other details that give the credibility or an illusion of one.

OSINT gathering starts with an in-depth look at the target's online presence (social media, blogs, public records, and so forth). Other useful information includes office geographical locations.

OSINT is particularly useful for remote offices or new branches of a company that have access to all the data but might lack the necessary security. he set of all the employee names and contact numbers and emails is also valuable to hackers.

Attackers learn the corporate language and culture so that they can fit into the role of an employee and any business partners or vendors that may relate to the target's network. They explore the technologies the company uses and any new software the company might have mentioned so that they can investigate the vendors' website for bug reports or possible weak spots.

Sometimes, companies make it easy for an attacker because they can manually type in the search term "company name" + password filetype:xls in the search engine and they will get an Excel spreadsheet that contains employee passwords. Some websites provide plenty of information. A hacker can look up server information such as IP addresses, DNS, and route information.

Shodan, aka Google for hackers, lists the vulnerabilities of a website. It allows you to track password dumpsites. Managing what is found on them is challenging; however, Kali comes with a tool "KeepNote," which supports the import and management of different sizes and types of data.

Once a tester identifies the targets with an online presence that are of interest, they work on the next step—identifying the IP addresses and paths to the target.

DNS reconnaissance deals with identifying who owns a specific domain or IP addresses; DNS defines the domain names and IP addresses assigned to the business or individual of interest and the way for the penetration tester/attacker to get to the target. The scary part is that the registrar may pick up on the attackers' search for the IP addresses and data, the target won't get the information, and the information that the target could directly monitor, like DNS server logs, is seldom retained or reviewed.

"Who Is" command is a tool to access IP address ownership identity. Depending on the database the response to a "whois" request will list names, addresses, phone numbers, and email addresses, IP addresses and DNS server names. It is a useful tool to find other domains hosted on the same server or operated by the same user. The attacker can use those other domains to gain access to the target especially if the domain is due to expire; they can seize the domain, and create a clone website to compromise visitors who believe to be on the original website

Authoritative DNS servers are the records for lookups of that domain, and they can facilitate DNS reconnaissance While there is an increase of third parties shielding this data, there are still plenty of online lists that offer domains and IP addresses assigned for government use. You can issue a whois command in Kali by entering whois in the main window: root@kali: ~#whois websitehere.com

On top of active reconnaissance, penetration testers use *passive reconnaissance*. Once the DNS information is in the attackers' hands, they can use brute force attacks to find new domain names associated with the target and to find misconfigured or unpatched servers, service and transport and port records.

Domain Keys Identified Mail (DKIM) and *Sender Policy Framework (SPF)* records control spam emails. If a hacker identifies records of DKIM or SPF, they are aware that this organization is security conscious.

Basic command-line tools like nslookup and Unix systems support additional command-line options such as dig. Sadly, these commands interrogate just one server at a time and require interactive and frequent responses to be effective.

Kali has several tools designed to query DNS information for a particular target easily. The tool selected has to accommodate the Internet Protocol version that is used for communications with the target—IPv4 or IPv6. The IP, or Internet protocol address, is a unique number used to identify devices connected to a public internet or a private network.

Kali includes multiple tools to facilitate DNS reconnaissance; dnsenum, dnsmap, and DNS recon. There are also large DNS scanners—DNS document enumeration (A, MX, TXT, SOA, wildcard) that can produce subdomain brute-force attacks, such as Google lookup, reverse lookup, zone transfer, and zone walking.

Some other common DNS terms include:

- Dnstracer determines where the selected domain got its information from and follows it back to the knowledgeable servers.

- Dnswalk checks domains for accuracy and consistency and attempts zone transfer only in brute-force attacks to obtain DNS information.

- DNSrecon obtains SOA record, MX (mail exchanger) hosts, servers sending emails, and the IP addresses in use.

There are no more free IP addresses in IPv4, forcing the IP addressing scheme to level up to IPv6. While it contains less than five percent of all IP addresses, the user engagement is increasing, so the testers have to know what the difference in the two entails.

Ipv6 has 128 bits and yields 2128 possible addresses. The increase in size might present problems to some penetration testers, but there are features of LPv6 that simplify these problems.

There is not as much support for functionality testing tools for IPv6, so the hacker has to make sure that tools are validated for accuracy. IPv6 is new, and because of this, the target may have some misconfigurations that will leak information. The hacker that can recognize this information and knows how to use it will conduct a more successful penetration test.

IDS, IPS, and firewalls might miss IPv6 because they are part of the older controls. Testers can then use tunnels to shelter communications with the network and exfiltrate the undetected data.

Tools that can take advantage of IPv6 in Kali are tools like Nmap. Route mapping was once a tool for diagnosis that allowed you to view the route of an IP packet. The TTL (time to live) in an IP packet showed an ICMP TIME_EXCEEDED message, decrementing the TTL value by 1 and counting the number of hops as well as the route that is taken. This shows the accurate path from the attacker to the target and identifies devices to access control and filter attack traffic.

Traceroute in Kali is a program that contains ICMP packets. There are also a few other tools to complete route traces such as hping3 - a TCP/IP packet analyzer.

2. Scanning

This step is used to understand how the target application responds to intrusion attempts using:

Static analysis – Scanning an application code to observe its behavior while the application is running.

Dynamic analysis – A practical way of scanning as it provides a live view into the performance of an application. It gives a detailed inspection an application's code while running.

The attackers face the most significant challenge while actively investigating; this challenge is the risk of identification, combined with balancing the need to map networks, investigate the operating systems and installed applications, as well as finding open ports.

To decrease the risk, they must stealthily scan networks. Manual scans are slow and ineffective, so tools such as Tor and various proxying applications that hide identity are incredibly useful. We go into a deeper analysis of scanning in chapter 8.

3. Gaining Access

After the scan and the newfound knowledge of the vulnerabilities, it is time to expose them by using web application attacks like cross-site scripting, SQL injection, and backdoors. Testers exploit these vulnerabilities in a variety of ways such as escalating privileges, stealing data, intercepting traffic, and so forth to expose the damage that a malicious hacker could cause.

There are tools available in Kali for development, activation, and selection of exploits to gain access. One of them is the internal exploit DB, and there are a few frameworks that simplify the use and management of exploits.

Metasploit Framework and Armitage is effective against third party applications. For an initial attack, the hacker generates a particular BMP file, and the victim needs to open the file in a vulnerable application. If the victim opens the image file in the vulnerable application, a meterpreter session is initiated among these two systems. The MSF prompt is substituted by the meterpreter prompt, and the tester can completely enter the remote system with a command shell. One of the first actions after the compromise is to establish that you are on the target system.

4. Maintaining access

This stage tests if the vulnerability can be used to achieve a constant presence in the system or at least long enough for a malicious hacker to gain in-depth access. A white-hat hacker imitates advanced persistent threats, which can remain in a system for weeks or even months and steal the fragile data of a business or an individual.

Once the attacker gains access, the malicious hacker's favorite part begins. This is when they reap the benefits and achieve the full value of their planned attack. The attacker performs a rapid assessment to scan the environment they are in. This means looking at things such as the infrastructure, accounts, target files, applications that can help attacks in the future, and the infrastructure. They locate the data files of interest, create additional accounts, and modify the system to help with the future attack strategies. They install the backdoors and channels to preserve control and communicate safely with the jeopardized system.

5. Analysis

After the results of the penetration test, a hacker writes a detailed report that includes vulnerabilities that are exploited, data accessed, and the amount of time the tester was able to stay in the system undiscovered Finally, this information is analyzed by security personnel to update and change solutions to application security and patch vulnerabilities to protect against attacks in the future.

Chapter 7: How Malware & Cyber Attacks Operate

Let's imagine a scenario where a client presents a file, and they are unsure if it's malware and what capabilities it has. In chapter 6, we went over the kill chain techniques, and when we go through a malware sample file, we are trying to find out what the malware is capable of.

Where does this malware fit in the kill chain?

Is it the initial patient zero machine that will go online and download more malware code? What is this malware's specimen capability?

Understanding what the malware is capable of is one of the main purposes of malware analysis or reverse engineering. You also have to ask: What is the attacker's intention?

If it's malware specifically for ransom, they are trying to encrypt for files and ask for money. If its purpose is to install other stolen PI data, then its intention is larger than just quick financial gain. Knowing the intention of the attacker helps you understand where else this malware is infecting your environment.

Types of Malware

Malware is a very general category, and there are few subtypes within it:

Ransomware

This malware is designed to freeze files and, as the name suggests, demand ransom from its victims in exchange for releasing the data; successful attackers realized that they could take it a step further by demanding money but not releasing the data. Instead, attackers demand another payment, and the cycle continues.

Paying up might seem like the only solution to dealing with ransomware, but the fact is, once you pay, the attackers will keep asking for more.

Adware

This is software that downloads, gathers, and presents unwanted ads or data while redirecting searches to certain websites.

Bots

Bots are automatic scripts that take command of your system. Your computer is used as a "zombie" to carry out attacks online.

Most of the time, you are not aware that your computer is carrying out these attacks.

Rootkits

When a system is compromised, rootkits are designed to hide the fact that you have malware. Rootkits enable malware to operate in the open by imitating normal files.

Spyware

Spyware transmits data from the hard drive without the target knowing about the information theft.

Remote Access Tool (RAT)

After your system is compromised, RAT helps attackers remain in your systems and networks. RAT helps criminals to obtain your keystrokes, take photos with your camera, and/or expand to other machines. One of the most dominant features of this type permits the malware to transfer all of this information from the victim to the attacker in a protected way, so you are not even conscious you are being spied on.

Viruses

A virus pushes a copy of itself into a device and becomes a part of another computer program. It can spread between computers, leaving infections as it travels.

Worms

Similar to viruses, worms self-replicate, but they don't need a host program or human to propagate. Worms utilize a vulnerability in the target system or make use of social engineering to fool users into executing the program.

The easiest way to evaluate the nature of a questionable file is to scan it utilizing automatic tools, some of which are available as business products and some as open ones. These utilities are meant to assess in a timely manner what the specimen is capable of doing if it ran on a system. They generate reports with details such as the registry keys utilized by the malicious program, its mutex values, file activity, and network traffic.

Fully-automated tools typically don't provide as much insight as a human examiner would when checking the specimen more manually. However, they help with the incident response process by rapidly handling large amounts of malware, allowing the analyst to focus on the problems that demand human observation.

Stages of Malware Analysis

There are a few properties of Malware Analysis, and in this section, we'll be looking at them one by one.

Static Properties Analysis

The first thing an analyst needs to do is take a closer look at the suspicious file by examining its static properties. These details can be obtained quickly because the analyst won't be running a potentially malicious program. Static properties include strings embedded into the file, hashes, resources, packer signatures, header details, and metadata like the creation date. Sometimes, looking at static properties can be sufficient for defining fundamental indicators of compromise. Static properties also help determine whether the analyst should take a closer look at the specimen using more comprehensive techniques.

Interactive Behavior Analysis

After the automated tool's done examining and the static properties' examination is complete, taking into account the setting of the research, the analyst can decide to take a detailed look at the malware specimen. A complete look means infecting an isolated system with the malware to observe its performance. The analyst needs to understand the malware's process and network activities, registry, and file system. They might perform memory forensics to understand how the program uses memory. The analyst tries to observe whether the specimen is attempting to attach to a distinct host, which is not available in the isolated lab. They mimic the system activity and copy the entire process to see what the malicious program does after attachment.

This approach to molding the lab to extract additional behavioral manners applies to files, registry keys, and other things related to the unit. Being able to utilize this level of power over the specimen in a properly arranged lab is what distinguishes this stage from automated investigation tasks.

Manual Code Reversing

Valuable insights are gained by reverse-engineering the code that compromised the computer. Some characteristics are hard and impractical to examine without examining the code. Insights that are only available through manual code are the logic of the malicious program, and there are capabilities that go beyond what's examined in the analysis of the behavior.

- *Disassembler* - This is a computer business that translates machine language into assembly language—the reversed operation to that of an assembler.

- *Debugger* - A debugger or debugging tool is a computer program that is used to test and debug other programs

- *Decompiler* - This is a computer program that uses an executable file as input and tries to create a high-level root file.

Reversing code needs a comparatively rare skill set and takes time. Many malware investigations don't comprehend or require the use of code. However, understanding how to operate at least some code reversing steps enhances the ability to assess the malware in the computer and understand the steps required to fight it.

Combining Malware Analysis Stages

The process of analyzing malicious software involves several stages, which we can list in the order of difficulty, and they are often represented in a pyramid-like scheme.

However, viewing these stages as discrete and subsequent steps simplifies the steps in malware analysis method a bit too much. Varying types of analysis tasks are twisted in one big malware analysis trial and error process, with the insights collected in one stage informing efforts conducted in another.

Now, let's see a bit about malware analysis systems, shall we? Here are the top 3!

Cuckoo Sandbox

Pros

- Automates the whole analysis process

- Processes high volumes of malware

- User-friendly

- Gets the exact executed code

- Can be very effective if properly used

Cons

- Expensive

- Parts of the code might not be triggered

- The environment could be identified

Google Rapid Response (GRR)

Pros

- Scales well

- Large setup

- Easy configuration

- Long-term supported

Cons

- Not very user-friendly

- Tedious

- Privacy implications

Yara Rules

Pros

- Simple

- Highly Effective

Cons

- Easy detection bypass

- Only does pattern/string/signature matching

- Expensive

Preventing Malware Attacks

In order to avoid malware, you should:

- Train yourself and other users on practices for avoiding malware.

- Don't download and run unknown software and don't blindly insert "found media" into your computer.

- Learn how to identify potential malware like phishing emails.

- Having unannounced exercises, such as intentional phishing campaigns, can help keep users aware and observant. Learn more about security awareness training.

Network security

Controlled access to systems on your organization's network and proven technology and methodology use like using a firewall, IPS, IDS, and remote access only through a VPN minimize the surface attack you are exposing your organization to. Physical system separation is usually deemed the last measure for most organizations and is still vulnerable to some attack vectors.

Use reputable A/V software

When installed, a suitable A/V software detects any existing malware on a system and then removes it. An A/V solution monitors and mitigates potential malware activity and installation. It is very important to be up-to-date with the vendor's latest definitions and/or signatures.

Perform routine security inspections

Scanning your organization's websites periodically for vulnerabilities such as software with known bugs and server/service/application misconfigurations will save your organization from potential malware attacks, protect the data of your users, and protect clients and visitors who use public-facing sites.

Create routine backups

A regular backup system in place is the difference between easily recovering from a harmful virus or ransomware attack and stressful, desperate scrambling with costly downtime/data loss. The solution here is to have regular backups that are verified and happen on a regular basis. Old, outdated backups don't restore correctly and are of no use.

Types of Attacks

Malware has many different forms and attacks in various ways. However, with some careful preparation and process developments, as well as ongoing user education, your organization can gain and maintain a solid security stance against malware attacks.

Cyber attacks

Criminal operations operating from the internet that are looking to gain financial or intellectual property are also known as cyber-attacks. Sometimes the objective of a cyber-attack is simply to disrupt the operations of a certain company. Sometimes a cyber-attack goes as far as state-sponsored attacks when governments of countries get involved in cyber-attacks to learn information on a geopolitical opponent or solely to convey a message.

By 2021, cybercrime damages are set to exceed $6 trillion! The annual Google profit is $90 billion. One trillion is one thousand times one billion, that's quite a bit of damage right there!

Phishing

A malicious hacker attempts to trick the victim into believing the hacker is a nice and trustworthy person in order for the victim to do a particular action. Perhaps the famous phishing scam is the "Nigerian Prince" where the hacker claims to be a wealthy Nigerian prince who needs your help in transferring funds to his account. In return, he offers you a promise of wealth once he gets back the access to his accounts. Just in the United States, these scams make over $700,000 a year! Unfortunately, as long as people keep sending money, hackers will use phishing scams.

Spear phishing attacks

Spear phishing involves personalizing the phishing email. So, while the "Nigerian prince" will send the same email to multiple addresses, the spear-phishing email will have a customized message making it look even more trustworthy.

Common examples of spear-phishing emails are those that look like they came from a bank (or a trusted source) where they ask you to enter login information because of a technical issue and clean up your account. Another example is a fake email from a supervisor, business owner, or CEO mentioning important company files. The spear-phishing email in this case contains a malware-infected Excel or Word file that, once opened, unleashes an attack. The hacker is interested in the company's data.

Unauthorized Disclosure

Whenever a company or an organization discloses information about you without asking for your permission, you have become a victim of an unauthorized disclosure. A medical provider leaking your health information is also an unauthorized disclosure.

Whaling

This is refined form of phishing because the hacker targets a high-value person like a CEO or a celebrity. The hacker gathers all the possible information about the target. They gather details about hobbies, passions, occupations, schedules, friends, family, and so on. They gather all this information so the victim truly believes the email is sent by someone trustworthy and thus clicks the link or opens an attachment.

Companies lose billions of dollars a year because of whaling.

Malware attacks and infections

Malware attacks are sent as malicious attachments or through downloads on suspicious website. The moment you open the attachment, the process of infection begins. Sometimes, it's possible for the malware to end up on your computer without your approval, although these cases are rare. They called these rare cases drive-by downloads.

Robust Cybersecurity and Information Security

The three pillars of security are people, processes and technology. This approach to security helps companies and organizations protect themselves from attacks and internal threats. Internal threats are when a user falls for a phishing scam or sends an email to an unintended recipient. Effective cybersecurity uses cost-effective risk management based on the likelihood of an attack or the worst-case-scenario.

People

Employees need to be knowledgeable about the prevention and reduction of threats and the role they hold in cybersecurity. The company needs to be educated and updated with the latest cyber risks and solutions to respond to attacks promptly.

Processes

Documented processes clearly define roles and responsibilities with specific procedures to follow when there is a suspicious email or any malicious activity. Processes are vital in communicating the organization's cybersecurity stance. They need to be reviewed and updated regularly for the latest cyber threats.

Technologies

Technical control is just as important as organizational measures. Installing antiviruses and accessing controls can decrease cyber risks or at least inform a hacker that the organization is aware of cybersecurity.

What Are the Consequences of a Cyber Attack?

Cybercrimes can cause significant interruption and destruction to even the most resilient organization. Affected organizations stand to lose their assets, reputation, and businesses, as well as face penalties and remediation costs.

Chapter 8: How to Scan Networks

The first phase of hacking is called footprinting. Footprinting is when an attacker gets information about a target. You can use this information for the next phase because footprinting alone is not enough; you only gather basic information. The additional details are gathered by a highly complex reconnaissance technique called scanning.

Network scanning is one of the most significant phases of intelligence gathering. You can gather information about distinct IP addresses that are available over the Internet, targets' operating systems and its architecture, and the services running on each machine. In addition, the attacker also collects details about the networks and their particular host systems.

If you have a substantial amount of information about a target organization, you have a bigger chance of learning all the weaknesses of that organization and of gaining unauthorized access to their network.

Scanning performance and the type of information gathered depends on the hacker's motives. The most common objectives include:

- Finding live hosts, IP address, and open ports of live hosts running on the network.

- Discovering open ports, which are the most desirable way to break into a system or network. Identifying open ports allows for an easy way to break into the target's organization network.

- Fingerprinting, or finding the operating systems and system architecture of the targeted system. The attacker launches the attack based on the operating system's weaknesses.

- Classifying the vulnerabilities and threats because every system has its weak spots and can be compromised by using them.

The most prominent risk of active surveillance is the target detecting the reconnaissance. With the tester's time and date imprints and the IP address source, the target victim can recognize the source of the incoming reconnaissance. Stealth methods are applied to decrease the chances of exposure. When applying stealth to maintain reconnaissance, a tester imitating the actions of a hacker uses a type of camouflage to avoid exposure or triggering an alarm. They can cover the attack within authorized traffic and adjust the attack to disguise the root and characteristics of incoming traffic. Hackers can make the attack undetectable by using encryption methods like modifying the source of IP, using anonymity networks, and modifying packet parameters with nmap.

Before the penetration tester (or the attacker) starts examining, they must ensure that all unnecessary services on Kali are disabled or turned off. It is possible for the DHCP (Dynamic Host Configuration Protocol) to interact with the target system when the local DHCP daemon is enabled. The DHCP can send alarms to the network administrators of the potential target.

Testers should disable IPv6 from running to stop IPv6 from announcing a foreign presence on the target network and to ensure that all traffic is routed first through an IPv4 proxy.

Modifying Packet Parameters

The usual approach to active reconnaissance is to perform a target scan, send defined packets, and use the returned ones to obtain information. Network Mapper is one of the better tools in the industry. Just like most of the applications that manipulate packages, nmaps must be run with root-level privileges to be effective. Network Mapper is why Kali defaults to root when you first install it.

Stealth techniques that help avoid detection and alarms include:

- Identifying the scan goal prior to testing and sending the minimum number of packets needed to determine the objective. For example, if you wish to verify the presence of a web host, you need to diagnose if the default port for web-based services, port 80, is open.

- Avoiding scans that attach to the target system. Do not ping the target or use synchronize (SYN) and unconventional packet scans such as reset (RST), finished (FIN), and acknowledge (ACK).

- Randomizing or spoofing source IPs, port address, and the MAC address.

- Adjusting the timing to slow down the approach of packets at the target site.

- Changing the sizes of packets by fragmenting packets or appending random data to complicate inspection from packet inspection devices.

Using Proxies Tor and Privoxy

The first step to understanding proxies and Tor is to understand onion routing.

Onion routing is anonymous communication over a network. In an onion network, messages are layered in layers of encryption just like the layers of an onion.

Tor produces free access to an anonymous proxy network and by encrypting user traffic, and then relaying it through a series of onion routing, enables anonymity. At each router, one layer of encryption is peeled to get routing information, and the message is then transmitted elsewhere. It protects against traffic analysis attacks by guarding the source and destination of a user's IP traffic. The Tor-Buddy script enables the frequency control every time the Tor IP address is refreshed, making it difficult to identify the user information.

Identifying the network infrastructure

Once the tester protects their identity, the next step is identifying the devices on the Internet-accessible part of the network. Attackers and penetration testers use this information to identify devices that might confuse or eliminate test results (e.g. firewalls and packet inspection devices). They also use this information to identify machines with known weaknesses and the requirements to continue with implementing stealthy scans. The idea is to gain understanding and knowledge of the target's focus on secure architecture and security.

Enumerating hosts

Host enumeration is when a hacker gains specific information regarding the host. The hacker needs to identify open ports, running services, supporting applications, and the base operating system, all the while being extremely careful not to be detected.

Live Host Discovery

Ping sweeps (ICMP sweep) are a basic network scanning technique. Ping sweeps are used to discover which IP's map to live hosts (computers). They are the first step to run against a target address space. Watch for responses that show that a target is live and capable of reacting.

To identify live traffic, hackers can also use:

TCP - The Transmission Control Protocol

- It provides virtual-circuit assistance.

- It manages flow control by ensuring packets are received intact and in order, checks for errors, and retransmits packets that are lost or damaged.

- The destination TCP module transmits an affirmation for every packet accepted.

- If the TCP module on the issuing machine does not receive the response, it retransmits the packet.

- If the acknowledgment is not received after numerous retransmissions, TCP assumes the data cannot be delivered and passes an error implication.

- There are no "negative acknowledgments" in TCP/IP.

UDP - The User Datagram Protocol

- UDP solely provides datagram service.

- The UDP module on the target machine can monitor for errors in packets, but it only delivers error-free packets to the application. Erroneous packets are discarded.

- The application must define the recipient address on every message.

- UDP is datagram-based, therefore every message is a discrete unit.

ICMP - The Internet Control Message Protocol

- Accountable for creating control messages.

- Includes instructional messages (slow down, better route, etc.).

- If sought, applications can interface with ICMP directly.

- It conveys an "echo" packet to a designated server machine via the ICMP protocol.

ARP - The Address Resolution Protocol

- ARP executes a "dynamic discovery" method of mapping IP addresses into hardware addresses, and it is normally used on Ethernet and local area networks.

- Before IP sends a packet to that network, ARP advises a local table to see if mapping exists between the objective IP address and the destination Ethernet address.

  - If it doesn't, ARP sends a broadcast packet asking the Ethernet the address of the machine with the given IP address.

  - Because it is a broadcast packet, every machine in the network gets it.

- The host with the requested IP address gives a reply, declaring its Ethernet address.

  - The originating machine gets the reply, adds an entry into its mapping table that connects the IP address with the Ethernet address, and sends the packet to its target.

To learn ping, you need to be capable of understanding TCP/IP packet. When a system pings, an individual packet is sent over the network to a distinct IP address. The packet carries 64 bytes, i.e., 56 data bytes and 8 bytes of data. The sender then waits for a reaction packet from the target system. A good return packet is expected solely when the connections are solid and when the targeted system is running. Ping can determine the number of hops between the two machines and the complete time it takes to complete the trip.

You can perform ping sweep using the Nmap Security Scanner. Ping sweep defines the IP addresses of live hosts. It permits you to scan many hosts at once and discover active hosts on the network. Several scanners can be operated from remote locations across the Internet to distinguish live hosts. Although the fundamental scanner is nmap, Kali provides many other applications that are also beneficial.

- alive6 and detect-new-ip6 IPv6 host detection.

- detect-new-ip6 runs on a scripted basis and identifies new IPv6 devices when added.

- PBNJ stocks nmap results in a database, and later conveys historical analyses to identify new hosts.

Kali Linux and Nmap Network Scanning

While Nmap isn't a Kali unique tool, it is one of the best tools for network mapping in Kali.

Nmap, or Network Mapper, is managed by Gordon Lyon, but many security experts use it all over the globe. The service works on Windows and Linux and is command-line (CLI) driven. Command-line driven means a program accepts special forms or letters as commands as opposed to a list of options in a menu. For those a little more hesitant with the command line, there is zenmap - graphical frontend for Nmap. Individuals should learn the CLI version of Nmap as it provides much more adaptability as opposed to the zenmap graphical edition.

What is the purpose of a Nmap server?

Nmap allows for an administrator to swiftly learn about the network systems just like the name Network Mapper suggests. Nmaps' ability to quickly find live hosts as well as services associated with that host add to its functionality. The functionality can be increased further with the Nmap Scripting Engine or NSE. This scripting engine enables administrators to immediately create a script that can be used to learn if a newly identified vulnerability exists on their network. Multiple scripts have been developed and included with most Nmap installs. Nmap is used by people with both ethical and malicious intentions.

Use extreme caution and make sure you are not using Nmap against systems where written permission has not been explicitly provided.

System requirements

1. Kali Linux

2. Another machine and permission to scan that computer with Nmap. This is often easily done via the creation of a virtual machine

3. A valid functioning connection to a network or if using virtual machines, a strong internal network connection.

First, log in to the Kali Linux and start a graphical session. A root password is necessary to log in so go ahead and type in your root password. Use a command "startx" so the Enlightenment Desktop Environment can be started; Nmap doesn't need a desktop environment, but we are going to be using Enlightenment here.

startx

Start Desktop Environment in Kali Linux. Open the terminal window. Click on the desktop background and navigate to the terminal: Applications - System - 'Root Terminal' or Xterm' or 'UXterm'

Launch Terminal in Kali Linux

For this tutorial, we are using a secret network with metasploitable matching and with a Kali machine.

Finding live hosts

Both of the devices are on a hidden 192.158.56.0 /24 network. The metasploitable machine we are about to scan has an IP address 192.158.56.102. while the Kali machine has an IP address of 192.158.56.101. If the IP address information was unavailable, a fast Nmap scan could assist in discovering what is live on this particular network. This scan is identified as a 'Simple List' scan (Sl command)

Nmap -sL 192.168.56.0/24

Nmap – Scan Network for Live Hosts

This scan didn't deliver a live host, and this can be because of the way certain operating systems manage port scans.

Ping and Find All Live Hosts on My Network

There are some methods that Nmap has ready to try to locate these machines. This next method tells Nmap to ping everyone in the addresses of the network 192.158.56.0/24

#Nmap -sn 192.158.56.0/24

Nmap – Ping All Connected Live Network Hosts

In this command, the -sn incapacitates Nmap's default behavior of trying to scan a port and a host and has Nmap attempt of pinging the host.

Locate Open Ports on the Hosts

To allow Nmap to port scan particular hosts, we could type in:

Nmap 192.158.56.1,100-102

Nmap – Network Ports Scan on Host

Let's say these ports all indicate some hearing service on this machine. Having many ports open on most machines is very strange, so it may be a smart idea to investigate these machines a little closer. Administrators could follow down the real machine on the network and look at the machine locally, but Nmap could do it much faster.

Find Services Listening on Ports on Hosts

To determine what service is listening to ports on hosts, we initiate a scan with Nmaps. Nmap examines all of the open ports and tries to banner grasp information from the services working on every port.

Nmap -sV 192.168.56.102

Nmap – Scan Network Services Listening of Ports

Nmap might have provided advice on what Nmap thought might be running on this particular port (highlighted in the white box). Nmap also tries to determine information about the running ports on this machine and its hostname. Scanning through this output could raise quite a few concerns.

For example, let's say the very first line claims that VSftpd version 2.3.4 is running on this machine; you can tell it could have weaknesses because this version is outdated.

Find Anonymous FTP Logins on Hosts

Let's have Nmap take a more intimate look at this distinct port and see what can we discover.

nmap -sC 192.158.56.102 -p 21

Nmap – Scan Particular Post on Machine

With this command, Nmap was directed to run its default script (-sC) on the FTP port (-p 21) on the host.

Checking for Host Vulnerabilities

Going back to the earlier example on VSftd having an outdated version, the vulnerability should raise some red flags. Try to check on VSftd vulnerability by typing in the following:

locate .nse | grep ftp

Nmap – Scan VSftpd Vulnerability

Nmap has an NSE script ready and built-in for the VSftpd backdoor problem. Run this script against the host and see what happens. To understand how to use the script type in

nmap --script-help=ftp-vsftd-backdoor.nse

Learn Nmap NSE Script Usage

You can use this script to try and see if this machine is vulnerable to ExploitDB issue identified earlier. Run the script and see what comes out:

nmap --script=ftp-vsftpd-backdoor.nse 192.158.56.102 -p 21

Nmap – Scan Host for Vulnerable

This machine is possibly a great candidate for serious research, and this doesn't suggest that the machine was compromised for malicious things, but it should bring some attention to the network/security organizations. Nevertheless, scanning an individually owned network in this form can be very slow. You can do a much more aggressive scan that can return much of the same data but in one command instead of many. Do note that an aggressive scan can trigger alarms!

nmap -A 192.168.56.102

Nmap – Complete Network Scan on Host

With one command instead of many, Nmap returns a lot of the information as it did earlier about the services, open ports, and configurations working on this device. Much of this information is useful in improving security and evaluating the software. There are numerous useful things that Nmap can do, but continue to use Nmaps in a controlled manner!

Chapter 9: VPNs & Firewalls

Threats to assets on the Internet are rising at a tremendous rate, so we must defend our networks from risks both known and unknown. One standard tool for accomplishing this task is a firewall. These networking products have grown a lot over the past several years. Simply preventing unwanted traffic and passing authorized traffic within networks isn't enough for today's firewalls. We require more than just packet filtering. We want serious security functions, such as Denial of Service (DoS) attack prevention and intrusion-detection systems.

What Is a Firewall?

A router that sits between a website and the rest of the network is called a firewall.

Firewalls are specially programed and are called routers because they connect to two or more physical networks, and they transmit packets from one network to another. They also filter the packets that move through the system administrator to execute a security policy in one centralized place.

Filter-based firewalls are the most manageable and most widely deployed types. These firewalls are configured with a table of addresses that identify the packets they will and will not forward.

Modern firewalls are separated into two categories.

- Hardware-based firewalls or appliances that use a particular hardware program.

- Software-based firewalls that use regular hardware and a regular OS, such as Windows NT Server 4.0, that's hardened, which means taken down to the bare essentials to minimize security threats.

Hardware firewall is defined as a physical device similar to a server that cleans traffic to a machine. Instead of plugging the network cable within the server; it is connected to the firewall, placing the firewall somewhere between the uplink and the computer. Like a conventional computer with a processor, memory, and sophisticated software, these devices also employ powerful networking elements (hardware and software) and push all traffic crossing that connection to examination by configurable sets of rules which allow or refuse access respectively.

Some common examples of known software firewalls are:

- Windows firewall

- UFW

- IPTables

- FirewallD

The hardware firewall is structured differently. The firewall is located outside your server and is attached straight to the uplink. If this is a newer setup, the firewall connects to your server. If this is a new setup to a production server, a maintenance window would be scheduled to handle the physical connection. Once the connection to the server establishes, all traffic going through the server goes through the firewall, requiring an inspection pass. This inspection pass allows you to have complete control over the type of traffic you're receiving, which is incredibly essential. Both hardware-based and software-based firewalls operate like network-protecting firewall software. Multiple companies use VPNs to ensure secure communication within the corporate network and end-users. Blending a VPN with a firewall is one solution to make administering the two functions more comfortable.

The problem with firewalls is that they are not able to differentiate the type of data they allow on your computer. You can do your best to adjust your firewall to allow only individual data packets that should apparently be harmless to pass through, but if any of these data packets are malicious, the firewall can't tell and will consequently let them through. A type of firewall that's designed to protect against malicious users intercepting a VPN connection is a VPN firewall.

There are hardware, software, and all-in-one firewall appliances with the objective of allowing only legitimate VPN traffic access to the VPN.

Consider a network with thousands of systems covering various operating systems, such as modified versions of UNIX and Windows. When a security defect shows up, each possibly affected system must be updated to fix that defect; this needs scalable configuration management and proactive patching to function efficiently. While challenging, this is plausible and necessary if using host-based protection. A widely accepted alternative or at least equal to host-based security services is the firewall.

The firewall is injected among the premises network and the Internet to build an established link plus to construct an outer security wall or border. The purpose of this border is to defend the premises network from Internet-based strikes. The firewall, then, provides an added layer of protection, shielding the internal systems from outside networks. This mirrors the classic military concept of "defense-in-depth," which is just as relevant to IT defense.

Entrusted computer systems are fit for hosting a firewall and frequently required in government applications. There are four common techniques in firewall practice to command access and implement the site's security strategy. Originally, firewalls concentrated primarily on service control, but they have since developed to provide all four:

- *Service control*: Defines the types of Internet services that can be accessed. The firewall filters traffic based on IP address, protocol, or port number; may present proxy software that accepts and interprets any service request before moving on; or may host the server software itself.

- *Direction control*: Defines the direction in which appropriate service requests may be admitted and allowed to flow.

- *User control*: Checks access to a service according to which user is trying to access it. This feature is typically used with users inside the firewall border (local users). It may additionally utilize incoming traffic of external users; the latter needs some form of strong authentication technology.

- *Behavior control*: Checks on how appropriate services work.

For example, the firewall may separate emails to reduce spam, or it may provide external access to only a part of the information on a local server.

A firewall establishes a single choke point that prevents unauthorized users outside of the preserved network, prevents possibly vulnerable services from joining or departing the network, and grants protection from numerous routing attacks as well as IP spoofing. A single choke point and the use of such a point clarifies security management because defense capabilities are incorporated on a single system or set of systems.

A firewall also presents a location for monitoring security-related issues. Reports and alerts can be executed on the firewall system.

A firewall is a useful platform for different Internet functions that don't relate to security, such as a network location translator. Network location translator uses a map to point out Internet addresses and inspects as well as logs users Internet usage. A firewall can serve as the platform for IPsec. A firewall using the tunneling protocol is a communications protocol that is the movement of information from one network to another. Tunneling involves giving the green light to a private network communication to send information across an openly accessible network, such as the Internet, through a process called encapsulation. It is a form of online camouflage because tunneling involves changing the face of the traffic data into a different one, possibly with encryption as a standard; it can hide if the traffic that is run through a tunnel is good or bad.

Because of the tunneling capability, the firewall can be used to implement a virtual private network; however, firewalls have their limitations:

- The firewall cannot protect against attacks that find a way around the firewall. Internal systems may have the dial-out capability to connect to an ISP.

  - They are called 'dial-out' calls because the user connects to a destination that is external to their

LAN over a dial-up telephone line! They are like those we used in the 1990s. An internal LAN can offer a modem pool that provides the dial-in capability for travelling employees and telecommuters.

- The firewall cannot fully protect against internal threats, such as a former upset employee or an employee who cooperates with an attacker against their will.

- A wireless LAN with weak security may be accessed from outside the organization. An internal firewall that separates portions of an enterprise network cannot guard against wireless communications between local systems on different sides of the internal firewall.

- A hacker can use portable storage like USB, laptop, or another device to infect and use externally, bypassing the firewall.

A firewall acts as a packet filter, stopping data on their way like security when you go to concerts. A firewall can work as a positive filter, allowing only packets that meet specific criteria to pass, like when security at a concert makes sure you have your ticket, or a negative filter, like when security at a concert makes sure you don't bring any weapons in. Depending on the firewall type, it may examine one or more protocol headers in each packet, the payload (the part that contains information) of each packet, or the pattern generated by a series of packets.

Packet Filtering Firewall

Packet filtering firewall has a set of rules determined for specific outgoing and incoming IP packets, and then it allows or denies the packet depending on if they follow the rules. The firewall is typically configured to purify packets going in both directions (from and to the internal network). The firewall filter rules are based on the information carried in a network packet:

Source IP location

The IP address of the source of the IP packet (e.g., 192.158.1.1)

Destination IP location

The IP address of the destination system the IP (e.g., 192.178.1.2)

Source and destination transport-level address: Port number and the transport-level

IP protocol field: Defines the transport rules and regulations.

Interface Firewall

Within three-plus firewall ports, the rules are based on matches to IP or TCP header. What this means is that if there is a match to its set of rules, the firewall decides right away whether to deny or permit access.

If there is no match to anything in this list of rules, then it takes one of the two default actions:

- Default = discard: If it's not specifically permitted, it means it's prohibited.

- Default = forward: If it's not specifically prohibited, it means it's permitted.

The workings of a firewall are more on the conservative side. The first rule is that everything is blocked, and the files can only be added on a case-by-case basis. This policy is more visible to users, who are more likely to see the firewall as an obstruction, and this is a policy more likely to be chosen by businesses and government organizations.

The default forward policy increases user-friendliness for end users but provides reduced security; the security administrator has to react to each new security threat as they learn about it. This policy may be used by more open organizations, such as universities.

An advantage of a packet filtering firewall is how simple it is and how packet filters typically are transparent and really fast.

The weakness lies in security because packet filter firewalls do not inspect upper-layer data; they cannot anticipate attacks that engage application-specific vulnerabilities or functions. A packet filter can only block some application commands but not all. If a packet filter firewall gives the green light for an application, all functions available within that application will be permitted.

With the limited information available to the firewall, there is a limited logging functionality. Packet filter accounts usually contain the same information used to make access control decisions (traffic type, destination and source address). Most packet filter firewalls do not support high-level user authentication settings.

Packet filter firewalls are vulnerable to attacks and exploits that take advantage of problems within the TCP/IP specification and network layer address spoofing. Many packet filter firewalls are not able to detect a network packet in which the OSI Layer 3 addressing information has been tinkered with. Spoofing attacks are generally orchestrated by intruders to pass the security controls in a firewall platform

It is not uncommon to base a firewall on a stand-alone machine running a common operating system such as UNIX or Linux. The function of a firewall can be executed as a module of a software in a router (LAN) switch.

Bastion Host

A firewall identifies bastion host as the most important and crucial point in the security of a specific network. The bastion host is a platform for a circuit-level gateway or an application.

The usual characteristics of a bastion host hardware platform are executing a secure version of its operating system, making it a hardened system, and installing only the services that the network administrator considers essential, such as proxy applications for DNS, FTP, HTTP, and SMTP.

Before the user is allowed any access to the proxy, a bastion host requires authentication. Every proxy service requires its own authentication as well. Proxy is configured and supports only a subset of the commands set. What does this mean? It means that a user can set a limited command set and apply them on to a few systems on the protected network.

Every proxy keeps a record and updates detailed audit information by logging all traffic, every connection, and the duration of that connection. The audit log is a necessary and very important instrument in detecting malicious attacks. Every proxy is a tiny package of software designed to implement network security. It is much easier to check them for vulnerabilities because they are very simple in design.

Every proxy is also an independent unit and doesn't rely on other proxies on the host. If there is a problem in one of them, they can be uninstalled and have no effect on the system and other applications.

Host-Based Firewalls

A host-based firewall is a module of software that is used to secure a specific host. These modules are available in many operating systems or can be provided as an add-on package. Like typical stand-alone firewalls, host-resident firewalls filter and restrict the flow of packets. Servers are common locations for these firewalls.

The advantages of a host-based firewall over a server-based are the customizable filtering rules and structural policies to implement. The security asks for external and internal attacks to pass through the firewall; they have an added layer of protection without the need to alter the firewall configuration.

Personal Firewalls

Personal firewalls control the traffic between a personal computer or workstation on one side and the Internet on the other side. They are typically used in home environments. Firewall functionality can be housed in a router that connects all of the home computers to a DSL, cable modem, or other Internet interface.

Personal firewalls are typically much simpler than either server-based firewalls or stand-alone firewalls. The main role of the personal firewall is to deny unauthorized remote access to the computer and then to monitor outgoing activity in an attempt to detect and block worms and other malware.

Distributed Firewalls

A distributed configuration of firewall involves host-based firewalls and stand-alone devices working together under one central administrative control. Tools let the administrators monitor security and set rules and policies across the whole network. They configure host-resident firewalls on hundreds of servers, and these firewalls protect against internal attacks and provide protection tailored to particular machines and applications. Stand-alone firewalls provide global security, including internal and external firewalls.

What Are Virtual Private Networks?

A virtual private network (VPN) is an example of implementing regulated connectivity over a public network such as the Internet. VPNs employ a concept called an IP tunnel—a virtual point-to-point link connecting a pair of nodes that are separated by several networks.

The VPN offers an elegant solution to network managers. A VPN is an assortment of computers that use special encryption and particular protocols, and because of this, it can connect through a relatively insecure network.

At databases, corporate sites, workstations and servers that are linked by one or more local area networks (LANs), the Internet or other public networks can be used to interconnect sites, providing significant cost savings. The use of a private network means wide-area management, which can require a lot more than the use of a private network and offloading the wide-area network management responsibility to the provider of a public network.

The problem with the public network is that it creates paths for unauthorized access due to the use of the networks available to the public. AVPN counters this problem by using authentication and encryption to provide a secure connection through an otherwise insecure network.

VPNs are usually more affordable than real private networks using private channels, but they rely on having identical authentication and encryption at both ends. Firewalls or routers can accomplish the encryption. IP or IPsec is the most common mechanism used for this purpose.

Understanding VPNs

Maybe the easiest method of understanding VPNs is to look at every word individually, and then tying them together.

First, there is the word "network." A network is a number of devices that communicate with each other through an arbitrary method such as printers, routers, or computers. The objects may be in different geographical locations, and the methods upon which they communicate are numerous.

The word "private" speaks for itself, and it is related to the idea of virtualization. Private means that the network communication is, in a way, a secret; the devices that are not participating in the communication are not privy to the content discussed. The other devices are unaware of the conversation altogether.

Another method of formulating the definition of "private" is looking at the word "public." A "public" facility is one which is fully accessible and is maintained within the terms and restrictions of a common public resource, often via a government or other public administrative entity.

In contrast, a "private" facility is where the access is limited to a strictly defined set of entities, and third parties do not have access. These types of private networks are any organizational networks which are not connected to the Internet. Outside connectivity doesn't exist, and therefore, there are no external network communications.

A VPN is a communications environment where admittance is regulated to permit peer connections only within a set community of interest and is formed through some sort of the partitioning of a common underlying communications tool, where this communications tool gives services to the network on a non-exclusive basis.

There are several motivations for building VPN's, but a common thread in each is that they all share the requirement to "virtualize" some portion of an organization's communications, or, in other words, to make some portion (or perhaps all) of the communications essentially "invisible" to external observers, while taking advantage of the efficiencies of a common communications infrastructure.

Types of VPNs

There are quite a few types of VPN, and in this section, we'll be going over all of them in order to give you an apt comparison.

Network layer

The network layer is in the TCP/IP protocol suite, and they consist of the IP routing system, which is how information is carried from one location in the network to the other. The "peer" VPN model is where the network layer forwarding path computation is performed on a hop-by-hop principle, where each node in the data transition path is a peer with the "next-hop node."

Traditionally routed networks are types of "peer" VPN models. The "overlay" VPN model is one in which the network layer forwarding path is done on the intermediate link layer network and used as a "cut-through" to different edge node on the other side of a great cloud.

Controlled route leaking

Controlled route leaking or route filtering is a system that consists of commanding route propagation. This model is a "peer" model since a router within a VPN site builds a routing connection with a router within the VPN provider's network, rather than an edge-to-edge routing peer relationship with routers in other places in that VPN.

While the basic Internet regularly carries the routes for all networks connected to it, this architecture implies that only a subset of networks forms a VPN. The routes connected with this set of networks are filtered and are not declared to any other set of associated networks. Given this lack of definite knowledge of position (other than other members of the same VPN), the privacy of services is executed by the inability of any of the VPN hosts to react to packets which include source addresses outside the VPN area of concern.

Virtual Private Dial Networks (VDPNs)

There are many technologies available for creating a virtual private dial network (VPDN), but they are divided into two principal methods: PPTP and L2TP.

PPTP Protocol

PPTP, or Point-to-Point Tunneling Protocol, is an old arrangement for executing VPNs. It is the simplest protocol to install. Users can remotely reach corporate networks from any Internet Service Provider (ISP) that carries the protocol.

PPTP VPN encrypts data with 128-bit encryption, which makes it the quickest but the most vulnerable.

Advantages of PPTP Protocol

PPTP is not only more affordable but also considerably easier to deploy than L2TP/IPsec and other VPN protocols. That's because it doesn't need Public Key Infrastructure (PKI) to run.

When you setup a VPN connection, it usually affects your Internet speeds due to the encryption process. Yet, you don't have to worry about this when using a PPTP VPN because of its low-level encryption.

Disadvantages of PPTP Protocol

The PPTP protocol is deemed to be the weakest as it only uses 128-bit encryption to guard your data. So, if you're administering with delicate information, you're better off opting for other VPN protocols that offer a substantial level of protection.

PPTP isn't the most stable VPN protocol when used on weak connections, and you'll often face performance problems! While it can be an adequate means of connecting employees and sharing documents, PPTP will let you down if you have a lot of private data that you need to share.

L2TP Protocol

L2TP, or Layer 2 Tunneling Protocol (L2TP), was created to provide a more reliable VPN protocol than PPTP.

L2TP is a tunneling protocol like PPTP that permits users to reach the common network remotely. L2TP VPN is a combined protocol that has all the characteristics of PPTP but runs a more high-speed transport protocol (UDP), hence making it more firewall-friendly. It encrypts data using 256-bit encryption and consequently uses more CPU resources than PPTP. However, the increased overhead needed to manage this security protocol makes it operate slower than PPTP.

Advantages of L2TP Protocol

The L2TP protocol is more stable than PPTP as it doesn't have any major protection vulnerabilities and uses the IPSec suite to provide end-to-end encryption, data origin authentication, replay protection, as well as data integrity.

If you want to setup L2TP on your machine, you'll be able to do so since multiple platforms come with native support for it. The L2TP protocol is very stable and doesn't face any performance issues when used on weak connections. This makes it a more reliable protocol than PPTP for setting secure connections to a remote network.

Disadvantages of L2TP Protocol

While using an L2TP VPN has its advantages, it also comes with certain restrictions. Since L2TP uses data twice, it demands a more powerful CPU processing, and you'll often encounter slow connection speeds. So, if speed is more valuable to you than security, using a PPTP VPN is a better answer.

Chapter 10: An Introduction To Cryptography & Digital Signatures

Cryptography means a method of protecting communication and information through the use of codes so that only those who are meant to receive the information can read and process it. "Crypt" means "hidden" or "vault," and "graphy" means "to write."

In computer science, cryptography is secure communication and information techniques that are derived from mathematical concepts. Cryptography is a set of calculations called algorithms that transform hard to decipher messages. These algorithms are used to form cryptographic key generating, digital signatures, and verifications. They protect information privacy, confidential communications (e.g. credit card transactions and email), and secure web browsing.

Techniques

Cryptology and cryptanalysis are the disciplines that relate to cryptography and techniques like microdots and image-word merging help hide information in transit or storage. In today's world, we associate cryptography with scrambling ordinary text (or cleartext) into ciphertext (with encryption) and then back again (decryption). Cryptographers are professionals in this field.

Modern cryptography follows four significant objectives:

Confidentiality

An individual could not explain or understand the information unless it were explicitly designed for them.

Integrity

The information in storage or transit cannot be tampered with, altered, or changed in any way without the detection of said alteration.

Non-repudiation

The sender cannot deny their intentions in the making or transmitting of the information nor at a later stage.

Authentication

The sender and receiver can confirm the identity of each other, the origin, and destination of the information.

Protocols that satisfy the above guidelines are called cryptosystems. While they are often mentioned in the mathematical and computer program procedures, cryptosystems also include the regulation of human behaviors like choosing complicated passwords and logging off unused systems.

Cryptographic algorithms are a set of procedures that encrypt or decrypt messages to secure computer system communications within devices such as smartphones as well as applications.

A cipher suite has a different algorithm for encryptions, message authentication, and key exchange. This protocol embedded process involves private and public key generation for data encryption/decryption, digital signing, and verification for message authentication.

Cryptography Types

Now, let's take a look at the cryptography types available to us!

Single/Symmetric - Key

Algorithms create a fixed length of block ciphers with a secret key that the sender uses to encipher data and the receiver uses to decipher data.

Advanced Encryption Standard (AES)

AES was founded in November 2001 by the National Institute of Standards and Technology as a Federal Information Processing Standard (FIPS 197) to protect delicate information. Universally used in the private sector, the standard is mandated by the US government. It was approved by the US government in 2003 for classified information as a royalty-free specification implemented in hardware and software globally.

AES is the replacement to the Data Encryption Standard (DES), and it uses longer key lengths like 128-bit, 192-bit, 256-bit to prevent hacker intrusions.

Public-key or asymmetric-key encryption is a public key associated with the originator for encrypting messages as well as a hidden key that only the originator knows (unless they share it or it's exposed). Types of public-key cryptography are RSA, DSA, ECDSA, and Diffie-Hellman key exchange.

After this, we'll need to map the data Hash functions (that return deterministic output from an input value) map data to fixed data size. Hash functions include SHA (Secure Hash Algorithm) -1, SHA-2, and SHA-3.

Cryptography History

Derived from the Greek "kryptos" meaning "hidden," cryptography dates from 2000 BC when the Egyptians practiced hieroglyphics. Hieroglyphics were complex pictograms full of hidden meanings whose exact message was known by only a select few.

Julius Caesar used the first modern cipher. He did not trust his messenger when communicating with his officers and governors, so he created a system in which every letter in his message was replaced by a character three positions ahead in the Roman alphabet.

In modern times, cryptography has become a battleground of the world's best computer scientists and mathematicians. Cryptography has been a crucial factor in success in war and business.

Governments do not want certain information to be available to the public or to leave their countries, so cryptography has been a subject of interest. However, because sending and receiving hidden information may be a threat to the national interest, there have been many restrictions.

The limitations of publicly distributed mathematical cryptography have been a controversial subject throughout the years. The Internet allowed the spread of robust programs and systems, so cryptography and advanced cryptosystems are now in the public domain.

Criminals can bypass cryptography to hack into networks that are responsible for data encryption and decryption and utilize weak implementations, such as the use of default keys; however, hackers have a harder time accessing data protected by encryption algorithms.

Raising concerns about the processing power of quantum computing to develop modern cryptography encryption standards motivated the National Institute of Standards and Technology to put out a proposal among the mathematical and scientific community for new public-key cryptography standards.

Quantum computing uses quantum bits (qubits) that can represent both 0s and 1s and consequently perform multiple calculations at once. While a large-scale quantum computer may not be developed in the next decade, the current infrastructure requires the uniformity of publicly identified and known algorithms that allow a secure approach,

There are three common types of cryptographic techniques:

Symmetric-key

The sender and receiver share a single key. The sender uses it to encrypt the plaintext and sends the ciphertext. The receiver applies the same key to recover the text. This concept is the most innovative in the last 300 years.

We are going to demonstrate how to make asymmetric encryption and decryption. In symmetric encryption, the same key is used for both encryptions of plaintext and decryption of ciphertext.

In short, to make asymmetric encryption, you should:

- Create a byte array from the initial password and a byte array from the primary key.

- Create a new SecretKeySpec from the key byte array using the AES algorithm.

- Create a new Cipher for the AES/ECB/NoPadding transformation and initialize it in encryption mode with the specified key using the getInstance(String transformation) and init(int opmode, Key key)

- API methods.

- Make the encryption, with the update(byte[] input, int inputOffset, int inputLen, byte[] output, int outputOffset) and doFinal(byte[] output, int outputOffset) API methods.

The result is a new byte array with the encrypted password.

- Initialize the cipher in decryption mode, using the same key.

- Make the decryption of the encrypted byte array. The result is a decrypted byte array:

```java
package com.javacodegeeks.snippets.core;

import java.security.Security;

import javax.crypto.Cipher;

import javax.crypto.spec.SecretKeySpec;

public class Main {

public static void main(String[] args) throws Exception {

Security.addProvider(new
org.bouncycastle.jce.provider.BouncyCastleProvider());

byte[] password = "JavaJavaJavaJava".getBytes("UTF-8");

byte[]                          pkey                          =
"keykeykekeykeykekeykeykekeykeyke".getBytes("UTF-8");

SecretKeySpec secretKey = new SecretKeySpec(pkey, "AES");

Cipher c = Cipher.getInstance("AES/ECB/NoPadding");
```

```java
System.out.println("User    password(plaintext):    "    +    new
String(password));

// encrypt password

byte[] cText = new byte[password.length];

c.init(Cipher.ENCRYPT_MODE, secretKey);

int ctLen = c.update(password, 0, password.length, cText, 0);

ctLen += c.doFinal(cText, ctLen);

System.out.println("Password         encrypted:         "         +
cText.toString().getBytes("UTF-8").toString() + " bytes: " +
ctLen);

// decrypt password

byte[] plainText = new byte[ctLen];

c.init(Cipher.DECRYPT_MODE, secretKey);

int plen = c.update(cText, 0, ctLen, plainText, 0);

plen += c.doFinal(plainText, plen);

System.out.println("User    password(plaintext):    "    +    new
String(plainText) + " bytes: " + plen);

}

}
```

Output:

User password(plaintext): JavaJavaJavaJava

Password encrypted: [B@64b045f4 bytes: 16

User password(plaintext): JavaJavaJavaJava bytes: 16

This was an example of how to make symmetric encryption in Java.

Public-key

Two related keys, the public and the private key, are in use. The public keys are free to distribute, while private keys are not. The public keys are used for encryption, and private keys are used for decryption.

So how does it work? First, the receiver generates 2 public keys n and e, and one private key d by choosing 2 large prime numbers p & q, such that n = p*q. You are choosing another prime number e, such that 3<e<n-1. Calculating d such that d*e-1 = k(p-1)(q-1).

Next, you're ready to encrypt. Transform the plaintext that you want to send into a number m, using the ASCII numerical representation or other methods. Encrypt the number m, by finding ciphertext c= m^e mod n. Send n, e, and c to the receiver.

Hash functions

No key is used in this algorithm. A fixed-length hash value is calculated and the plain text that makes it unlikely for the contents of the plain text to be obtained. Hash functions are also utilized by many operating systems to encrypt passwords.

"Integer obj1 = new Integer(2009); String obj2 = new String("2009"); System.out.println("hashCode for an integer is " + obj1.hashCode()); System.out.println("hashCode for a string is " + obj2.hashCode());

It will print hashCode for an integer is 2009; hashCode for a string is 1537223

The method hashCode has different implementation in different classes. In the string class, hashCode is computed by the following formula:

s.charAt(0) * 31n-1 + s.charAt(1) * 31n-2 + ... + s.charAt(n-1))

where s is a string and n is its length. An example:

"ABC" = 'A' * 312 + 'B' * 31 + 'C' = 65 * 312 + 66 * 31 + 67 = 64578"

Signatures

Allows sender verification, avoidance of sensitive information sending, and it's a significant aspect of encryption. It is the capacity to sign a message.

How to Sign a Message

Generate a signature M, such that $S = M^{\wedge}d \bmod n$, and transfer S along with your message. Remember that d is your private key.

How to Verify a Signature

The customer can immediately establish that the signature is valid if $M = S^{\wedge}e \bmod n$.

R code on Github to sign & verify a message.

Hashing

You'll notice in the sample code above, I used a function sha256() for a variable m_hash. Hashing is a one-way cryptographic function that allows you to irreversibly transform information into a string of letters and numbers called a hash. Hashing is different from encryption because a hash is meant to be impossible to decrypt, although many have tried and some have succeeded. When you hear about a password or other security breach, it is usually referring to a cryptographic hack in which hackers have been able to match hashes back to the original text.

The primary use of hashing is in password verification. It would be very hazardous for your bank to keep a database of passwords, so it maintains a database of hashes that match to your actual password. When you log into your bank account, the system hashes your password and then checks it into the hash that it holds a file for you. This system runs because hashing algorithms provide the same hash for the same password—hashes are not a random combination of characters.

It is crucial to have unique and complicated passwords because if I hash the password "password123" and match it up to hashes that correspond then, I know you chose "password123," and I can log in to your accounts.

Rainbow tables

We talked about rainbow tables in earlier chapters, but how do they work? Take your credit card PIN codes. There are 10,000 combinations of 4-digit PIN codes using digits 0–9. A rainbow table would present the hash for each of the 10,000 codes, and a hacker could utilize this list of hashes to map the hash back to your code, thus decoding your PIN from its hash. Banks and most other organizations realize that hackers want to acquire sensitive information, so they typically implement an extra layer of security through "salt."

Salts are extra strings of characters added to a password (or other information) to make it extra unique, longer, and more challenging to hack. Instead of having a PIN of "0000," attaching salt would exchange your PIN to something like "0000B_of_A_salt," which would have a completely different hash.

Organizations can use salts to make hacking remarkably tricky. To use a rainbow table to crack such an algorithm, you would need a rainbow table for every potential salt, adding excessively to the number of potential combinations of PINs.

Blockchain

Cryptography permits blockchain to authenticate senders in a network through signatures, as well as guarantee that prior transactions and records, known as "blocks," cannot be exchanged.

Blockchain also employs hashing algorithms to assign a different hash to each block, enabling you to distinguish among blocks.

Digital and electronic signature difference

Electronic signatures, or eSignatures, encompass many possible types. Digital signatures are a specific technology implementation of electronic signature. Both digital signatures and other eSignature solutions permit you to sign documents and authenticate the signer.

There are differences in purpose, technical implementation, geographic use, and legal and social acceptance of digital signatures versus other types of eSignatures. In particular, the use of digital signature technology for eSignatures varies significantly between:

- Canada, the United States, UK and Australia - countries that support open, technology-neutral eSignature law

- Most countries in the European Union, South America, and Asia - countries that support tiered signature models

Digital signatures, like written signatures, are unique to each signer. Digital signature solution providers, such as DocuSign, develop a specific protocol, PKI (public key infrastructure).

PKI requires the provider to practice a mathematical algorithm to generate two large numbers, called keys. One key is public, and one key is private.

When you sign a document electronically, that signature you are creating is using a private key. The algorithm acts as a cipher. The cipher creates a hash matching the signed document. The result is the digital signature. That signature is then stamped with the right date and the exact time of the document signature, and if the document changes after the original signature, it becomes invalid.

For example, imagine you sign an agreement to sell a timeshare using your private key. You send the document to the buyer, along with a public key. If the public key your buyer received can't decrypt your signature, it means your signature is not yours or the agreement has changed since signing. That signature is now invalid.

PKI requires the key creation, conduction, and the services of a Certificate Authority for security. DocuSign meets PKI requirements for a safe digital sign.

Creating Digital Signatures

DocuSign offers quality digital signature technology that makes it easy to sign digital documents. DocuSign provides interface for signing documents online and working with Certificate Authorities.

Certificate Authorities is an entity that issues digital certificates that certify ownership of a public key by the named subject. It is an authority responsible for issuing SSL certificates trusted by web browsers. You might be required to supply specific information depending on the authority you are using. There could be restrictions and limitations on who the recipients are and the order they are sent in.

DocuSign's interface guides you throughout the process and guarantees that you meet all of these conditions. When you receive a document for signing via email, you need to authenticate as per the Certificate Authority's terms and then "sign" the document.

Industries and countries already have eSignature standards as well as CAs for business documents. Follow the local standard and work with trusted CAs by using PKIs to help prevent forgery or changes to documents, making your business security operation top of the line.

eSignature is legally enforceable. The EU directive for eSignatures and the United States passed the ESIGN Act (Electronic Signature in Global and National Commerce Act). These acts make electronically signed documents legally binding, just like the paper-based contracts. Most other countries have accepted the same laws, and many companies have improved compliance with the industry regulations.

Chapter 11: Hacking As A Career

Ethical hacking is a way of helping computer professionals and administrators in their attempts to secure networks. The underlying theory associated with ethical hacking is simply that of a completely new path to security.

Ethical hacking is really penetration testing and entails penetrating the devices and systems just like a malicious hacker would, but for purposes of security.

The demand for cybersecurity professionals jumped up over 7% in the last year because of the number of high-profile breaches. The exciting thing is that there is not enough job seeker interest. The results are top dollar offers and a high demand for workforce. If you're thinking about a cybersecurity profession, you are in the right time to do so.

The problem with job listings is job postings that are seeking specific skills that are only received from being trained on the job, so young people tend not to have experience and click less on the postings.

If you've been looking at getting some good money, then cybersecurity might be your field!

The highest-paid job titles in cybersecurity in the US include:

Chief Information Security Officers

Salary: $100,000-$500,000

Every senior-level executive is well-paid, and so are the CISOs. They are valuable to companies because they have to be business savvy with exceptional technical skills. They manage the incident response team and oversee engineers. Their role doesn't stop there; CISOs are responsible for the company data privacy, threat prevention, and revenue protection. CISO reports to the CTO or directly to the CEO. A median salary ranges from $135,000 with the chance of $100,000 in bonuses and profit-sharing.

Senior Security Consultant

Salary: $76,000 - $160,000

Senior security consultants analyze security setting and find safer practices, procedures, tools, and software. They modify and analyze firewalls, software, and hardware like routers. Their role allows them to lead security training for employees, participate in meetings for cybersecurity advancement, and partake in risk analysis. They are the ones to implement security standards across devices. The average salary is around $105,000, with the possibility of commissions, profit sharing, and bonuses making the high end of the pay around $150,000.

Security Engineers/Security Team Leads

Salary: $60,000-$180,000

Security engineers work on preventing or minimizing impact breaches. They secure systems, install firewalls, as well as encryption programs. Security engineers hunt vulnerabilities and respond to security incidents.

The role entails helping security awareness, overseeing a small development team, mentoring new developers, and communicating with management.

Security engineers typically report to a unit leader, or a software manager or director, who in turn communicates to the CISO. Security engineers typically earn around $130,000, with the opportunity of additional compensation varying from $2,000 to $40,000 in bonuses and profit-sharing.

Data Security Analyst

Salary: $46,000 - $170,000

A data security analyst protects sensitive data such as billing information, credit card information, and customer data. Their focus is on the cloud servers where they determine what data can and should be stored in locations that are as vulnerable as a cloud server. Data security analysts report corrections and weaknesses for the IT security to follow up on and analyze accessed data to discover who accessed it and when and where it was accessed. A median salary for data security analysts is around $120,000.

Penetration Testers

Salary: $47,000 - $130,000

Penetration testers look for weaknesses in the company's system before the malicious hackers find them. They look for weak passwords, security awareness within the company, and act like a malicious hacker to report on vulnerabilities.

Penetration testers payrolls vary broadly based on expertise level, business, and region, with a broad range of $45,000 to $135,000.

Emerging Cyber Security Positions

Cybersecurity is continuously evolving, and as such, the new roles are always emerging. Some of the new positions include a business process security consultant, cloud security architect, IT auditor, security awareness trainer, and many more. For cybersecurity, the new jobs are continually emerging, and the old ones are always evolving.

Often, promising cybersecurity job candidates come across cybersecurity roles accidentally, but it is becoming challenging to find knowledgeable candidates due to the increasing demand for workforce and the low supply of candidates. The online searches that lead to most clicks are "Information technology," "Amazon," and "Engineer."

Other highly-clickable links are "Security," "full-time," "entry-level," and "government." There are job seekers with related interests out there, but the employees need to broaden the horizons when it comes to employment in this field. The industry is not as open to hiring women as it could be. Young people tend to find themselves out of a job because companies are always looking for people with experience, which most of the graduates don't have.

What Is the Best Entry-Level Cyber Security Position?

For the best chance of employment in a specific company, do thorough research on the exact job requirements. For some security specialists, certain certificates may not be required, but when you are just starting out, they are an excellent idea to work toward while you're gaining some experience, and they can help you when it comes to promotion. Some certification options are EC-Council Network Security Administrator (ENSA), Cisco Certified Network Associate, Certified Information Security Manager, Certified Information Systems Security Professional, and CompTIA's popular base-level security certification.

A security specialist is a fantastic way to enter the cyber-security field. Gather as much knowledge as possible about what companies are looking for employees and all the major rob requirements. These requirements vary amongst the employers, and you could miss the opportunity to build up your knowledge before applying for jobs.

How to Become a Security Specialist

Everyone needs protection from something. It is the world we live in, and we accept it as a daily thing. We didn't talk to strangers when we were children; we have insurance on our houses, cars, and health. Company data needs protection from strangers lurking online, waiting for an opportunity to steal it, and that's where security specialists come in handy.

Career Path

There are positions you start out in and then work your way up the ladder. There are many routes to take when you start as a security specialist. From security specialist, you can work your way toward security manager, IT project manager, security consultant, or security architect.

Finally, you can branch into a security officer or director. There are a few job postings that fall under other titles that are classified as security specialists, so if you are looking for an entry-level security specialist job, you may also look for titles such as network security specialist, computer security specialist, information security specialist, and IT security specialist.

Requirements

- Knowledge in SIEM (security information and event management)
    - SIEM provides real-time analysis of security alerts generated by applications and network hardware.
    - Ability to execute penetration tests

- Complete understanding programs and software such as anti-malware, antivirus, and firewalls

- Fluency in Java, C++, C# or C

- Knowledge of Unix, Windows, and Linux systems

- Confidence in coding

- Load Balancer, Proxy Server, and Packet Shaper knowledge

Of course, every employer is looking for skills such as self-motivation, teamwork, communication skills, and problem-solving.

There are a few personalities known in the cybersecurity industry for their business or hacking skills. For anyone looking to advance in the ethical hacking career, these are people to follow:

Raj Samani

The chief for McAfee who has assisted multiple law enforcement agencies in cybercrime. He is a special advisor to the European Cybercrime Centre in The Hague. Samani is a recognized contributor to the security industry and has won many awards such as Infosecurity Europe Hall of Fame and Intel Achievement Award. He is the co-author of the book called *Applied Cyber Security and the Smart Grid* as well as the technical editor for other publications.

Kevin Poulsen

Former black hat-hacker Poulsen was one of the creators and developers of SecureDrop, an open-source software platform for secure communication among journalists and sources. It was originally formed under the name DeadDrop.

After his friend's passing, Poulsen launched the first instance of the platform in *The New Yorker*, on May 15, 2013. Poulsen turned over the expansion of SecureDrop to the Freedom of the Press Foundation and joined the foundation's technical advisory board.

Samy Kamkar

He is a hacker, whistleblower, entrepreneur and security researcher, and a high-school dropout. At the age of 17, he founded Fonality, a communications company based on open-source software that had $46 million in private investments.

Graham Cluley

Cluley is a British defense blogger and writer of grahamcluley.com, a daily blog on the newest computer security news, theory, and information.

Cluley began his profession in the computer security business as a programmer at S&S International, where he drafted the first Windows version of Dr. Solomon's Antivirus Toolkit.

From 1999 to 2013, Cluley was a senior technology consultant at Sophos and also worked as the head of corporate communications, spokesperson, and editor of Sophos's Naked Security site. In April 2011, Cluley was enlisted into the InfoSecurity Europe Hall of Fame.

Georgia Weidman

She is a serial entrepreneur, security researcher, trainer, speaker, author, and penetration tester. She has a master's in computer science and CISSP, CEH, and OSCP certifications. She is currently creating Penetration Testing 2, an updated training manual on penetration testing with all the new techniques for security specialists.

Brian Krebs

He is an American investigative reporter best known for his coverage of malicious hackers and cybercriminals. He is the author of a daily blog KrebsOnSecurity.com, where he covers cybercrime and security with all the updated news from the industry.

Joseph Steinberg

Steinberg is an advisor at Emerging Technologies and a recognized leader in the industry. He led businesses and divisions related to the information security industry for over two decades, and he is amongst top cybersecurity influencers globally. He has written books ranging from *Cybersecurity for Dummies* to the official CISO certification exam study guide.

He is one of just 28 people in the world to hold the advance information security certifications CISSP, ISSMP, CSSLP, and ISSAP. He possesses a rare knowledge of information security, and his inventions are cited in over 400 patent fillings.

Rebecca Herold

She is the CEO of The Privacy Professor consultant firm and president of SIMBUS, the information security, privacy, and compliance cloud services. She has written over 15 books and contributed to hundreds of others. She led the NIST Smart Grid Privacy Subgroup for several years, and she is the co-founder of IEEE P1912. She was also a professor at Norwich University and received numerous awards. She appears regularly in the news including in KCW123 morning shows and hosts a radio show "Data Security and Privacy with the Privacy Professor."

Brian Honan

He is a well-known business expert on data security, specifically the ISO27001 information security model, and has addressed plenty of major conventions relating to the management and securing of data technology

Dmitri Alperovitch

He is a computer security industry administrator. He is co-founder and leading technology leader of CrowdStrike. In August 2011, as vice president of warning research at McAfee, he wrote Operation Shady RAT, a report on Chinese intrusions into at least 72 organizations, including businesses, organizations, and government agencies all over the world.

Robert Herjavec

Herjavec applied for a job at Logiquest trading IBM mainframe emulation boards. He was underqualified for the job but persuaded the firm to give it to him by volunteering for six months. To pay the rent during this period, Herjavec waited tables. He eventually became general manager of Logiquest. He established BRAK Systems, a Canadian integrator of Internet protection software, from the basement of his home and sold to AT&T Canada for $30 million.

Herjavec established Herjavec Group in 2003, a security solutions integrator, reseller, and operator. He is currently the CEO, and the firm is Canada's fastest-growing tech company. The firm has grown from 3 to 150 employees, and sales rose from $400,000 to $500 million in 5 years. His company's growth rate is over 600%.

Conclusion

The influence of information technology and the increasing dependency on technological support infiltrates almost all of today's society. Some concern arises from the apparent lack of security integrated inside information technology and network systems. Of particular importance is our increasing dependence on the Internet and networking abilities. The Internet has presented us with vast opportunities in a broad array of areas that were not possible or even thought achievable in previous years. In modern times, we are able to access vast amounts of knowledge and combine the newfound knowledge in modern ways. Along with the actual skills given by the Internet and networking, the negative aspects also infiltrate in unforeseen ways.

While crime existed long before the internet, the Internet and information technology have led to cybercrime coming into our homes and businesses in unthinkable ways. Perpetrators of today have a new stage for conducting activities, and people are so puzzled at the subsequent onslaught from these endeavors that, in many cases, only reactive actions may be implemented.

Kali Linux is one of the many programs out there that helps us in the constant fight—it could even be called a war—with malicious hackers. To fully use all the advantages it offers, we could spend years in training and development, but with a little research, anyone can learn just the basics of cybersecurity. The first step is always smart clicking, updating software, and staying educated on security awareness. Once you are fully aware of how essential cyber-security is, you can start making your personal and company data less accessible to one of the many scams, viruses, and dangers in the internet world.

Understanding VPNs, malware, and firewalls can drastically improve the chances of your business surviving in the ever-changing online world. Today, cybersecurity causes trillions of dollars in revenue loss, and preventing malicious attacks could mean the difference between your company becoming one of the sad statistics or overcoming, adapting, and rising stronger after being hacked.

Ethical Hacking

A Beginner's Guide to Computer and Wireless Networks Defense Strategies, Penetration Testing and Information Security Risk Assessment

Zach Codings

Introduction

Let's think back to a little over 10 years ago. The whole field of IT security was basically unknown. Back in the '90s, there were barely any professionals who could say they worked in "cybersecurity" and there were even less of those that actually knew what the area was about to become.

Security was essentially just anti-virus software. You know, that annoying popup which screams at you every time you try to get a file off the Internet. Sure, packet filtering routers and similar technologies were also popular, but it wasn't really seen as, well, important in the slightest.

The concept of a hacker at the time was more akin to the hacker memes we have today. It came mostly from movies that Hollywood made...or just referred to someone that got a low score while playing golf.

It was ignored. Nobody really saw hacking as much of a threat. After all, what was there to gain at the time? It was seen as mostly an annoying triviality that might pop up every now and again. Today, we understand it is a massive threat that can impact multi-billion dollar corporations and even our governments.

It was ignored, and at the time, it was obvious why. Unfortunately, later on the whole IT industry would feel the impact that hackers can leave. These days, the number of IT system security professionals is over 61 thousand around the world. This isn't for no reason. In fact, the field of cybersecurity is not only growing, but growing at a faster pace than the already-growing tech industry according to the ISC. There are now more security companies out there than anyone really cares to remember and trust me, most of them do work that's much more important than a mere antivirus.

Cybersecurity has even seeped into the mainstream, with countless people authorizing things through their firewalls and using VPN's every day to watch videos unavailable in their location.

There are so many ways to address any security problems that it can be a true headache to think about it. Heck, even just considering the alternatives of a single program is enough to give you a migraine from the sheer amount of competition out there.

Since the 90's, the world has changed massively. I mean, think about the last day you spent without using an electronic device. Chances are you don't even remember that. So, what does all this change carry for your home? For your computer? Does it mean you're thrust into a dangerous world every time your computer, phone, or any other smart device is as much as turned on? Well, that's pretty much what it means, as every single one of those changes led to the world and the criminals in it changing to meet the new surroundings, too. In the digital world, you will find a playground which is padded with mines that need but one single touch to explode, if they even need that much. Even the simplest of things can spell quite a bit of trouble for you.

If you ever plug into the internet without a decent firewall, there is a certain chance that your system will get hacked in mere minutes.

Whenever you open an unassuming email from friends or family, there is always that chance that the email will open a backdoor to your system. This means that it will take a hacker very little time to gain access to even the most private parts of your computer.

If you use your Internet Messaging program to download and execute a file, you should not be surprised if your desktop turns into a virus hot zone.

Even when you are browsing through trusted websites, you are completely open to hacker attacks. When this happens, your sensitive files are at risk of being taken or deleted. Sadly, the fear of being a target of an online drive-by is often more than a fear and you can be targeted completely out of the blue. It is not a rare occurrence.

More often than not, people like to spread the word on the dangers of cyber-terrorism. The fear, uncertainty, and doubt that people generally feel when it comes to this subject are, however, anything but unjustified. People are often blind to how high the chance of a digital cataclysm actually is. Organized crime and terrorism have their finger everywhere, and this includes the digital world, too. Several organized terrorist cells are often raided. When their computers are found, the majority of what's on them is cyber-hacking plans and similar files that depict how they would attack the infrastructure of the United States.

You might remember August 14, 2003. This was the day when the biggest power outage in the history of the United States happened. Around 20 percent of the U.S. population was left without power for more than 12 hours. It is very easy to make yourself believe the most light-hearted narrative and say that some trees fell or strong winds damaged some part of the network. While this explanation might be correct, think about this: 3 days before the power outage, the Microsoft Blaster worm was unleashed on the Internet. This worm is known to be one of the most dangerous and volatile worms ever made. While this might have been a coincidence, one can not help but be just a tiny bit skeptical.

You might be thinking that all of the fear and heaviness caused by cyber-terrorism is not justified. You might think that since nothing happened so far, nothing will. But think about this: nobody expected 9-11 to happen. Everybody knew that there was a safety risk when it comes to airport security and terrorism, yet nothing was done about it.

The skepticism is understandable and welcome, as some skepticism is never a bad thing. But you should trust me when I say that cyber-terrorism is a very dangerous yet likely thing. You should trust the media when they start panicking about small cyber-attacks because that's how it all starts.

You should be careful when it comes to this. A hacker is like a burglar. They try to poke away at your safety until they can pin-point a place from where they can enter your safe space and take your valuables. Every second of the day there are hacker groups and organized criminals that are digging away at your safety. You should never let them succeed. Nobody should ever sit back and watch another person take what they hold dear and desecrate their safe space. Help yourself by learning more about this, and use the resources that are available to you in order to protect yourself as much as possible.

While increasing your security might seem like something straight out of movies, I assure you that it is something that you can do quite easily. It's more about what you think than anything else. You can compare it to working out or studying. As long as you are adamant and have a schedule on which you do certain things, it will quickly become a part of your life. If you don't integrate it into your day-to-day schedule, you will quickly start to forget it and find excuses not to do it. Security is a process and not a goal. So, it's important for you to make it a part of your routine and soon enough, you are going to be able to do it without thinking about it.

If you avoid this, however, you will be hit sooner or later. The best thing that you can do for yourself now is to educate yourself and get some knowledge on the subject. You can't protect yourself from something you do not understand, and protect yourself from it you must. It is not your right to protect yourself, but your duty. Getting to know something that might be dangerous for you is the best thing you can do to keep yourself safe. If you fill the gaps in your knowledge, you will be able to prepare yourself for most things.

What is well known and plain to see is that you are going to have to always keep track of it in order to protect yourself from malicious users everywhere. This is where the know-how in this book comes in and saves the day. It will give you a way to implement the technology available to us currently and the knowledge that has been accumulated over the years to keep your systems secure for a while. Keeping your system safe is impossible unless you get into the mind of the malicious user and use the knowledge that you obtain while doing so. See which tools they use and use the same tools to see the weaknesses in your system that they could see if they were targeting you. Unless you do this, any other assessment of how secure your system is can be very inaccurate.

Ethical hacking encompasses many different legal and safe activities. It is necessary to improve systems all across the globe and make them safer. The activities include, but are not limited to, white-hatacking, vulnerability testing, and penetration testing. While the benefits of this kind of activity are relatively hard to see, if you look into it a bit more, it becomes clear as day. The only way to improve and keep up with the changing times is to improve yourself. This is done by testing your system and improving upon the results that you get from the testing. The book mainly covers what it means to be an ethical hacker and how you are supposed to do this correctly in order to find effective countermeasures and close any back doors that your system might have in order to keep malicious hackers out of it.

Who is This Book For?

First of all, it is important to emphasize the fact that should you choose to use the knowledge provided by this book for malicious activities on your own, the blame is all on you. No one else who was associated with you gaining the knowledge is not to blame, nor are they liable for the way that you use the knowledge. The contents of this book can be used by white hat hackers (ethical hackers) and black hat hackers (crackers) alike. The book gives such a close look into the cracker mentality that it becomes a good source of study for crackers themselves. The methodologies in the book can be used both ways. The responsibility of using the knowledge correctly falls on you completely. You should always use it in authorized ways.

To be an ethical hacker means to focus your efforts on detecting security holes that might have been overlooked and find ways to fill up those holes. Whichever kind of testing you run on your system will help you out to manage and improve your system, as well as any other system you might do this for. Computer security is nothing to scoff at. It is an issue that should always be taken seriously.

The same can be said if you are doing this for another individual. Your aim is to protect their system from malicious users and plug in the holes which seem to be the most problematic. If you read this book correctly and soak up all of the knowledge, you will always be on your A-game when it comes to computer security. You will enjoy the feeling of being self-sufficient in that regard and will also bask in the glory of being a helpful individual to anyone that has concerns with computer safety. No matter what kind of system we are talking about and how far advanced that system is, there are always going to be hundreds if not thousands of possible ways to crack it.

This book will help you understand the following:

- The results of several important and impactful case studies made by several different experts on the subject

- Different hack attacks that are widely used in the cracking community and all of the nuances that lie beneath

- The countermeasures that you can take to protect yourself

In order to be prepared for the tasks yet to come and be able to properly hack your systems, you should get to know the info in

Part 1 of the book. There is an old adage that says: "If you fail to plan, you plan to fail." This is very true about hacking, especially when it comes to the ethical part of it. There are several steps you need to take before you can start working. You need to get permission from the owner of the system first and develop a general game plan on how you are going to approach it. Some may look at the information in this book and say that it is made to turn script kiddies, people who use automated tools to crack into systems with little to no technical knowledge, into actual hackers. This, however, is wrong. The knowledge presented in this book is provided to you for ethical purposes. You are supposed to use it to hack your own systems or the systems you have permission to hack in order to make the system itself more secure and the information on the system safer.

There are some chapters you can skip in this book. For example, if you are not using a Windows operating system, then there is no point in reading the chapters that detail how to use them.

The book goes into the explanation assuming a few things:

- You have an average grasp on concepts and terms that are related to information, computer, and network security

- You can differentiate ethical hackers from crackers

- You have a computer and a network that you can apply these techniques to

- You can access the Internet and get the tools that might

be necessary for some of the jobs

- The owner of the system gave you permission to use the methods and techniques from the book.

The book is divided into seven parts. You should get well-acquainted with the format, as you might need to jump around from one part to another. Each of these chapters gives you different methods and techniques that will help improve your ethical hacking skills.

The Difference Between Ethical Hacking and Cracking

For a long time, there has been a great deal of controversy regarding the term "hacker". The general populace automatically assumes that a hacker is someone who does the line of work in an unethical way and aims to hack into systems for their own gain. This, however, was not always the case.

Before hacking became a wide-spread criminal activity, the word "hacker" had a very positive meaning. It was used for the best of the best when it comes to programming. The likes of Linus Torvalds were proclaimed to be hackers. This image of the word changed very quickly when outbreaks of cybercrime started happening. The media took it upon themselves to clear up the happenings while muddying the names of the finest programmers at the time. The programming community was outraged at this and many fiery debates started erupting over the subject. Many influential names from both of the communities rose up to give their input. But, alas, it was all for nothing. The narrative that the media pushed was already widely accepted by the public and it was too late to change it. The word "hacking" was labeled as a negative one. This was not helped by the cracking community enforcing the narrative that hacking is strictly a malicious activity. The people in the cracking community like to carry the title of "hacker" with great pride. This is seen as an insult by the programming community, as a hacker should be a title only given to those that have shown great expertise when it comes to programming.

There are several parallels that need to be drawn in the discussion. While the cracker subculture is a part of the programming community, the programming community aims to stifle and denounce any efforts made by the cracker subculture. This is where the term "cracker" came from. The programming community sees crackers as the most dangerous and heinous individuals. In order to prevent as many people as possible from using the term "hacker" for these individuals, they took it upon themselves to find a new term to replace that one in the narrative. This is where the term "cracker" comes into play. Once the term was coined and generally accepted by programmers, it was immediately pushed into the media. Great efforts were made to clear up the difference. While it, at first, appeared as it was going somewhere and that some change was on the horizon, in the end, it fell into the water. The media was adamant on pushing their narrative and, on top of that, people from the cracking community started calling themselves hackers.

Programmers generally use this differentiation and call malicious hackers crackers. Some people outside of the community stick to it too, but the majority of the public was already influenced to the point where the damage is irreversible. Still, it is important to make the differentiation. It is imperative that we never forget about it, as there are great names such as the aforementioned Linus Torvalds whose names are always connected to the term "hacker".

What you should keep in mind is that hacking is like any other trade. A parallel is always drawn between it and locksmithing. Why? Because the main principles of the two are fairly similar. Hackers try to find weaknesses in the system, but this is legal if it is done with good intentions and the permission of the owner of the system. The act of lock-picking is considered highly illegal and is a crime of its own, but a lock-smith needs to do it from time to time in order to satisfy their clients' needs. Imagine being stuck outside of your own house and leaving the keys on the inside. You don't really want to break down the door or damage your windows, so you call a locksmith to help you break into your own home, as funny as it may sound. Hacking works on a similar principle. While the act itself can be illegal, you will always want the help of an experienced hacker when you are working on improving the security of your system.

It is a fact that hackers, white hat hackers to be precise, are necessary for the industry today. Many corporations and organizations offer classes and payrolls for skilled hackers. Why? A computer system is like an organism. You build up immunity by getting sick. The situation is similar with computer systems. The only way to really improve your security is to suffer an attack. A weakness becomes very apparent once somebody abuses it. Today, many companies hire skilled hackers in order to improve the security of their systems. Most hacking attacks happen in a pattern. If you perform an attack on your system and adjust your system to be able to prevent such an attack in the future, it will be able to prevent all of the attacks of the same kind or at least slow them down. However, only the most skilled are hired for these jobs. You would not want an inept doctor treating your illnesses. Hence, you don't want an inept hacker to fiddle around with the delicates of your system. The individuals who do this line of work are usually deemed to be hackers by the whole of the programming community. This is the most respectable thing you can do with your hacking skills, as it takes a great deal of expertise and it is done for a good cause.

When we are talking about the different kinds of hackers it is important to point out that there are categories based on the legality and legitimacy of their activities, rather than the level of skill they possess. Based on this, we have the following categories:

White hats - White hat hackers are hackers that good-intentioned programmers want to be. They work to keep systems safe. They find weaknesses in the system and find ways to remove them. The line of work white hats have is usually very well paid and they are considered to be one of the most valuable technology assets. The work done by white hat hackers is not illegal. White hat hackers have the permission of the owner when they start working on a system.

Black hats - Black hat hackers are your typical crackers. Their work is usually fueled by malicious intentions and selfishness. They work to crack a system in order to find data that they or someone else might want. This is considered to be highly illegal and is the reason that the word "hacker" has such negative connotations. They do the same thing as white hats, but out of malicious reasons and without the permission of the owner. There is a sub-group of black hats called script kiddies. No one in the community likes script kiddies, not even black hats themselves. Why? Because script kiddies have almost no skills in the line of work and use pre-scripted tools to do all of the work.

Grey hats - Grey hat hackers fall somewhere in the middle of the spectrum. Their activities are illegal, but they do not steal or destroy the data, rather they do it for sport. They usually contact the owner of the system they cracked in order to offer them a fix for the vulnerability.

The Hacker Ethic

There are two rules that make the difference between crackers and actual hackers. The two rules were made regarding the legality and legitimacy of the hacking process. They are the following:

1. Information-sharing is good for everyone. Every hacker has the duty to share their knowledge. They do this by writing open-source code and helping people to improve their systems as much as possible.

2. Using one's knowledge in order to crack systems for fun and practice is alright as long as no illegal activities are done through this activity.

These principles are widely employed, but not by everybody. Most hackers work under the first ethic by writing open-source software. This is taken a step further by some more extreme individuals that believe that all information should be available to everyone. The GNU project stands behind this philosophy and believes that any kind of control over information should be considered bad.

The second ethic is usually considered to be a tad more controversial, as there are individuals who consider that any kind of cracking should be considered immoral and illegal. What separates grey hats from black hats is the fact that they do not use their expertise to destroy or steal information. This is why they are considered somewhat benign in the community. There are several rules of courtesy among hackers. Once a grey hat hacker cracks into someone's system, he should always contact the owner of the system itself in order to tell them how the attack was made and how the system can be protected from similar attacks.

Almost all hackers are willing to share their knowledge and expertise on the subject. This is the most reliable way that the two ethics manifest. There are huge networks that work as places where the community can gather and where individuals can exchange experiences and tools, as well as techniques and tips.

Chapter 1: What is Ethical Hacking?

Cyber criminals present one of the biggest problems somebody can find in the digital worlds. There was a time when hackers weren't taken as seriously, but things changed drastically in the past several years. In India, for example, there are many companies that pay hefty sums of money to hackers in order to protect some of their sensitive and valuable information. It was reported back in 2013 that 4 billion dollars were lost by Indian companies during that year alone due to cyber attacks.

As the world of business evolves and becomes more and more technologically dependent, many companies were forced to enter the digital ecosystem and adopt the technologies that the ecosystem offers in order to function more efficiently. The need for more efficient ways to protect information is becoming more and more prominent due to the threat of more and more intense and damaging breaches of security. All of these changes made the shortage of talented people in the information security sector apparent.

Nasscom reported that the need for white hats far surpassed the number of white hats they had in 2015. There were 15,000 certified ethical hackers in India, versus the 77,000 that were actually needed.

What is Ethical Hacking?

Ethical hacking is the practice of using hacking techniques in order to help out systems with protecting the important information stored on it. This is a new league in the IT-sphere of programming which is gaining more and more recognition. This line of work employs people in order to hack into security systems and locate weak points in them and find a way to fix them.

The techniques employed by white hats and black hats are very similar and usually the same. The difference is that white hats need to make improvements to these techniques in order to stay on top of the more malicious counterparts in the line of work. Corporations that use security systems and work with huge amounts of sensitive information hire white hat hackers in order to prevent malicious individuals from accessing the information stored on the system. A white hat hacker's job is to hack into the system of the employer in order to locate the parts of the system that are at risk and fix the holes. The first step that every white hat takes is called penetration testing. This is a way to find vulnerabilities in systems. It is an easy way to assess the strength of the system.

Ethical hacking includes many services. Some of these are:

- Application Testing: Detects the flaws in a system

- Remote or war dialing: Tests modem connections

- Local network testing: Works to analyze the work of protocols and devices in the system.

- Wireless security: Checks the overall security of the entire framework.

- System hardening: Strengthens the system and fixes the holes in the system

- Stolen laptop: This is done through the PC of an employee that has access to a bit of information. It checks the personal information stored in software.

- Social engineering: Uses the personality of the hacker to gain access to a system.

The Need for Ethical Hackers

As I have mentioned a few times, cybercrime is becoming more and more of a big deal. Crackers are becoming more and more sophisticated. They also gain access to more and more funding due to the many malicious organizations that want to steal information from important sources.

Every day, businesses need to improve their own systems in order to get with the advancements in hacking tactics and techniques. Hackers find hidden vulnerabilities in computers more and more often, so in order to protect your system, you will always have to improve your security. This is the same for every corporation that handles very sensitive information. White hats are usually well-trained professionals who work towards improving these systems.

Some traditional companies have a problem when it comes to the understanding of white hat hacking. The banks in India have often faced vicious hacking attacks that cost them a great deal of money. Their lack of faith in the benefits of ethical hacking led to their defenses against cybercrime being quite minuscule.

There is a malware called "darkhotel" which hit hotels and several other parts of the industry. This proved that the industry was falling behind when it comes to cybersecurity. The malware itself was used to gather information on people of interest that reside within the hotels by using the hotel's Wireless Network access.

The cracking community constantly grows when it comes to tools and techniques. New kinds of malware, worms, and viruses are made every single day. Due to this, businesses are becoming more aware of the benefits of ethical hacking and how it can help protect their networks.

The bottom line is that owning an enterprise in this day and age is as risky as it could be due to the number of malicious users that have access to so many different tools. This is why every system should be tested on a regular basis in order to keep up with the times. There is a holistic approach that is involved in the assessment of a system due to the complexity of the field of computer and network security. There are many interactions and operations that are involved in any security system and some of them might be very fragile. Ethical hackers are the best people to do this. They are individuals with the ability and know-how that can help anyone fine-tune their system.

How is Ethical Hacking Different from Cracking?

As I have stated a few times, the techniques that all hackers use are similar, if not the same. The tools and techniques used are universally accepted by all of the people that involve themselves in this activity. The only difference between ethical hackers and others is why they are doing what they are doing. Crackers, or black hats, are fueled by their own selfish and malicious reasons like profit or harassment. The efforts of white hats are made in order to prevent the black hats from taking advantage of systems.

There are several other things that can help you differentiate black hats from white hats:

The goal of the activity: While it is true that white hats use all of the techniques that have been developed by black hats, they do this in order to help out an individual or corporation. This is done in order to determine how a black hat would approach the system in order to spot flaws and help fix them.

Legality: The main differentiation between ethical hackers and crackers is the fact that, even though they do the same thing in the same way, only one side is legally acceptable. White hats have the consent of the system's owner before doing it, while black hats break the law by doing it without the owner's knowledge.

Ownership: White hats are hired by different companies to help them out with improving their systems. Black hats do not hold ownership over the system and they are not employed by somebody who does.

Roles and Responsibilities of an Ethical Hacker

The ethical side of hacking is no simple thing. While white hats are often regarded highly in the programming community, as well as among business owners, they are still regarded as criminals by many. The very activity is considered to be immoral by many. Many white hats prefer not to have the connotation of "hacker" next to their name due to the reactions they may get.

In order to keep their practices legal and prevent others from viewing them as criminals, white hat hackers need to be well acquainted with their responsibilities and stick to the guidelines. The following rules are some of the most important for white hat hackers:

- An ethical hacker is always supposed to ask for the consent of the owner of the system before starting to get into it. You will need the approval of the owner for every activity that you do on the system and you are expected to provide the information you gained through your activities to the owner.

- Once the hacker analyzes the system, he must make his findings and plan known to the owner before taking action.

- The hacker must notify the owner of what was found during the search.

- The hacker is expected to keep his findings and activities confidential. Due to the nature of ethical hacking which is helping the security of a system, the hacker should not disclose the information to anyone else.

- Remove all of the found vulnerabilities after finding them in order to stop black hats from entering the system without authorization.

In order to be successful in the line of work, you are going to need a certain set of skills. The knowledge a white hat hacker needs to possess is both wide and deep. It needs to encompass several parts of the computer technology field and needs to be highly detailed. Some of the skills that are needed are:

- Detailed knowledge of programming - Any professional that works in the fields of Software Development Life Cycle and application security is required to possess this knowledge.

- Scripting knowledge - This kind of knowledge is important to anyone who works on host-based attacks and network-based attacks.

- Networking skills - Most threats to the system come from networks. Due to this, you will need to know about all of the devices that are connected to the network and how they interact with it.

- Knowledge about different platforms used on different kinds of devices

- Knowledge on how to use hacking tools and techniques available on the market

- Knowledge on servers and search engines

Chapter 2: Hacking as a Career

It is safe to say that identifying yourself as a hacker will make a few heads turn and give you some unpleasant stares, as people who do not know the difference between black hats and white hats will immediately assume that what you are doing is highly illegal. No matter what you are doing, whether it's helping out a branch of the military in order to improve the security of the classified information, or hacking into a school's database in order to see what loopholes can be abused by unauthorized users in order to gain access to the data, your efforts will usually be frowned upon to a certain extent by others. People will usually assume that you work as a part of an underground society of vandals and consider it not to be a valid career choice.

This is everything but true. Hacking can make a career unlike any other. In order to properly work as a certified ethical hacker, you are going to have to go through a bunch of prep work and training. A diploma or certificate regarding computer security is not always required, but it is always nice to have. What you will need is extensive knowledge of the subject. Knowing how computers work and interact with one another is the most important part when you are looking to get into the line of work. A lot of movies and TV shows like to show hacking to be something glamorous. They never show everything that goes into the line of work. Experience and knowledge are big deals when it comes to hacking, which is sometimes easily overlooked.

With that in consideration, if you did all of the learning on your own by using your systems, this line of work can be more challenging than it might have appeared to be at first.

If you had practiced using your own equipment, the next logical step is freelancing, where you can get some more experience and some endorsement for your activities. As you may expect, however, hacker freelancing isn't exactly the most stable position ever, so you might experience some serious lows when it comes to finances. It is a great way to gain more experience and some cash on the side. It is also a great way to build up an impressive resume. Freelancing is usually a great place to start.

After you have gained a substantial amount of experience, you should start sending job applications to tech companies to see if your experience is needed. You can send applications to many big firms. This is smart, as they tend to pay more for these services. However, there are many smaller companies which will be more eager to hire you, and are ready to pay a bit more for your services if you are good enough. Always keep your sights open, as you can find work in this industry if you have the skills.

Being an ethical hacker is quite a challenging line of work due to the fact that a proper white-hatacker needs to know everything about systems and networks. This is why certain organizations started to give out certifications that support talented hackers when it comes to work. Aspiring ethical hackers have been looking into getting these kinds of certifications as proof of skill.

There are several certifications that give some big benefits. Some of these benefits are:

- Hackers with these certifications have the necessary knowledge to build and maintain security systems. If you prove to be good at this field of work you will be a great asset to any organization that might look to hire you.

- Hackers with these certifications have an increased chance to get higher salaries. A certified ethical hacker can hope for a salary of $90,000.

- It validates your efforts and makes it easier for you to get a job in companies and makes you more noticeable among your peers.

- Most organizations prefer certified individuals when it comes to system security due to the growing needs of the field.

- Startup companies look for certified individuals. These companies pay quite a penny for individuals that do these jobs.

The Different Kinds of Ethical Hacking

When it comes to ethical hacking, there are several kinds of practices that are employed. Due to the outstanding variety of possible cyber attacks, every company wants to test as many possibilities as possible. This is why they employ individuals with different degrees of knowledge. These are the so-called boxes. There are three kinds.

Black Box Ethical Hacking

Black box ethical hackers know nothing about the organization whose systems they are trying to get into. These people do not have a focus on a particular part of the system or a particular method. They use all of the tools at their disposal in order to crack the system. The attacker has no focus due to the fact that he has no information on the organization he is attacking.

White Box Ethical Hacking

White box ethical hackers are concerned with how much time and money will go into a job. When a white box ethical hacker starts working on a system, they know everything about the organization. They are used to emulate an attack that could be executed by someone close to the company or inside of the company. These attacks target the specific parts of the system in order to strengthen them. The drawback of this method is the fact that the hacker will attack the already known vulnerabilities and possibly overlook other vulnerabilities.

White box ethical hackers usually cooperate with teams of different people from Human Resources, Upper Management, and Technical Support Management.

Grey Box Ethical Hacking

Gray box hacking is somewhere between the previous two. It combines the two attacks. It has a certain amount of information on the company, but that information might change from time to time. It has the same drawback of white box ethical hacking due to the obvious vulnerabilities.

The History of White Hat Hacking

Ethical hacking is not a thing of the new age. It has been around for a long time under different names. The first documented instance of ethical hacking happened when the United States Air Force executed what they called a "security evaluation" of their systems. The Multics operating system was tested in order to see if it could be used to store top-secret files and documents. During this test, it was determined that Multics is better than the other options that were available to them, but it was still lacking and had many vulnerabilities when it comes to security which could be exploited with not much effort on the side of the cracker. The test was made to be as realistic as possible as they believed that this is the only way to get precise results that can be considered proof. The tests varied from simple information gathering to full-on attacks that endangered the entire systems. Ever since then, there have been a few more reports of the US military doing these kinds of activities.

Until 1981, white hat hacking was not known as a term to many people, but it was then that The New York Times introduced the term and labeled it to be a positive kind of hacking tradition. There was an employee in the National CSS that wrote a password cracker software. When he decided to disclose this software he was met with great outrage. The company was not angry at the existence of the software, but at the fact that he kept the existence of the software hidden. In the letter of reprimand the NCSS stated that the company sees the fact that employees finding security weaknesses as beneficial to the company and that the company encourages it.

Dun Farmer and Wietse Venma were the first to see the potential of white hat hacking. They were the people who turned it into a technique that can be used to assess the security of a system and improve it later on. They pointed out that, after a certain time, once they have gathered a certain amount of information, they could crack into a system and deal a great amount of damage to it should they choose to do so. When they talked about what can be done through white-hat hacking, they gave several examples about how information can be gathered and exploited, and how, using this knowledge, attacks can be prevented. They made an application from all of the tools that they used during their research and made it available for download to anyone who might be interested. The program is called the Security Administrator Tool for Analyzing Networks, also known as SATAN. The program saw a great deal of attention from the media in 1992.

Chapter 3: Making Money Freelance

Ethical hacking is a huge field. The amount of jobs available is huge, which leads to them paying more and more as time goes on, as there aren't enough ethical hackers in order to cover all of these positions at all times.

In my opinion, the best way to earn money with ethical hacking is by going freelance. In this chapter, we'll be going over the pros and cons of doing freelance work, as well as how well you can expect to earn, and the process of becoming a freelancer.

What Is Freelancing?

Freelancing is basically becoming a company yourself. While you don't have to set yourself up as a CEO or anything, it does serve to paint a good picture. A freelancer is basically a one person company. You'll need to be your own marketing, your own PR, your own accountant, and your own employee. This takes a lot of grit, so if you're someone that's satisfied with a regular, 9-5 job, then I'd advise against going the freelance route. On the other hand, if you're someone that wants to try very hard, get to the top of the field, and rake in ludicrous amounts of money, then this area is for you.

Freelancing basically means abandoning the traditional concept of employment and becoming something of a full-time contractor. You'll need to pick your own clients, as well as find them yourself. This can be quite difficult for beginners, though we have a few great ways listed out below.

As a freelancer, you can also dictate your own hours, which is great. If you're an early riser, then you can start work at dawn, but if you're a late owl, nobody will judge you for starting your work day at 4AM. This also means you don't have to do all your work at once, and can segment your work so that you only work for the time that you're actually productive.

You'll also only get paid for the stuff you do, so make sure to reflect this in your hourly rate. It's not uncommon for freelancers that are in an area that usually pays $20 an hour to command $30 an hour or higher rates. Freelancers are also usually considered to be more competent than in-house employees, so make sure your knowledge reflects this.

Finally, going freelance means abandoning any concept of job security. Clients will come and go as the wind, however, if you're able to keep a steady stream of them, you'll make a lot more than your in-house counterpart.

The Pros and Cons of Going Freelance

Let's look at what you'll be getting from becoming a freelancer first, shall we?

Pros

First of all, you get freedom, in more than one sense. The most important ones being location and time. You can work from anywhere you want. This is what caused the "digital nomad" lifestyle to crop up. That is where you abandon a constant physical location, and simply travel the world with your freelance income backing you.

This is a great way to live, and many people have whole-heartedly adopted it because of how comfortable it is to know that you can literally always just switch locations and go somewhere new. Having the freedom to go on an adventure whenever you want is extremely exciting.

On the other hand, this also has much more mundane applications. Has your day ever started badly because of your morning commute being cluttered or annoying? Well that's never going to happen again because your commute...doesn't exist! You just get out of bed...wait nevermind, you just lay IN your bed and work. This kind of freedom is generally unavailable to anyone but the richest in society, however, with freelancing, it's pretty easily possible.

Other than that, work often digs into your time when you don't want it to. This means that, for example, you wanted to go out with a friend at 9 a.m. but because of work, you were unable to. If you were a freelancer you wouldn't have this issue, as you'd be able to simply move all of your work to later in the day, and still go out with your friend. This also means that sometimes, if you had a really terrible day (eg. someone broke up with you), you can take a day off from work, as long as you make up for it later.

This is also great for productiveness, as everyone has different hours within the day that they consider themselves to be productive in. Rather than trying to fit into a company's working hours, you get to pick and choose your own.

The 2nd reason you should consider freelancing is money. Successful freelancers make a LOT more money than their desk-job counterparts. For example, some of the most successful freelance ethical hackers are raking in amounts that are in excess of $500,000 a year. Let that number sink in. On the flip side, it's not like the lead ethical hackers at companies aren't earning a lot, but it's usually not even half of that.

Obviously, this has some caveats. If you're getting employed by the FBI, you'll probably get offers that will put any freelancer to shame, but in order to get employed by the FBI you would have had to have a huge portfolio of freelance work beforehand.

For this reason, if all you're looking for is money, I'd suggest you consider freelancing much more strongly than working at a desk job position.

The 3rd reason to go freelance is, well, fun. Now, don't take me as one of those people that consider all work to be fun, but if you're a freelancer, you get to pick your opportunities.

Do you know that feeling when your boss assigns you a task you really hate, and you have to do it even though you'd rather do double that time, just working on something else? Well, as a freelancer, you don't have to do it. If there's a specific area of ethical hacking that you really dislike, then you can simply avoid it and never interact with it again in your life.

This freedom also lets you take bigger and better challenges. You don't have to wait for your boss to trust you with a task that they reckon is above your abilities. Just take it and give it a try! Worst case scenario, you don't live up to the client's expectations and your reputation takes a bit of a temporary hit.

Cons

The first con to freelancing is, well, the freedom. But wait, you say, didn't you say freedom was a pro? It is, if you can bear with it. It can be extremely easy to fall into the trap of not working enough, as you're not bound by contract, location, or anything similar.

This often leads to "freelancers," people that are actually unemployed, and have been holding onto their last job title and stapling freelancer next to it in hopes of making it sound better. After all, with nothing to chain you down, it can be very easy to fly too close to the sun.

The second pitfall (relatively similar to the first) many fall into is late assignments. Starting with the first time you say "Oh yeah this is going to be late" then everything henceforth cascades endlessly. From one assignment to the next. This can often even happen without agitating clients, but doing things at the last moment is generally a bad idea if for no other reason then for the stress that it causes. The stress itself often causes issues which cascade, meaning that if one day you were just a bit stressed out, the next you might be quite stressed, and afterwards you're having a meltdown.

Now, the third is finding clients. Finding clients is...hard, especially for those just starting out. In fact, if you're in a higher-class country (UK, US, Russia, etc.) then you might find that most entry-level jobs in your field of choice are paid under rate. While most freelancers do earn more than their desk job counterparts, this relationship flips on its head when it comes to entry level positions.

After all, an entry level job can usually be done just as well by someone from India (which has a low average wage) and someone from the US. Luckily, when it comes to ethical hacking, there are far more jobs than there are freelancers. This means that this kind of freelance rate depreciation doesn't really happen.

On the other hand, even if there are so many jobs, that doesn't mean it isn't difficult to reach clients, and that they aren't selective. Getting your very first freelance job is always really hard, which is why I'd recommend going for a desk job at first, at least until you've gotten your feet wet in the industry. This is because generally, when it comes to finding clients, people rely on experience. Freelancers will want to work with people connected to their past clients, and their past clients will be looking for freelancers with experience. As a general rule of thumb, experience is king in the freelancing world.

This brings us to another con of freelancing. Being your own boss is surprisingly hard. You need to be able to make your own website and make sure to advertise yourself. You need to pay attention to SEO as well as your skills in the actual field you're working in. While freelancing is a job that has very free hours, in a way, it's a 24/7 job in the sense that you never really get to stop working for a while.

How to Start Freelancing

Now, assuming you've gone past the pros and cons of freelancing and have decided to start, what do you need to do?(If you've decided it isn't for you, feel free to skip this part.)

Now, I'd like to split this up into two parts. In one of them I'll be recommending a road to someone that already has IT experience, while in the other I'll be gearing the text towards a complete novice.

I Have Experience, Now What?

Now, if you have experience, you've got a leg up on pretty much everyone that doesn't. The first thing you should do is make a website.

A website? Shouldn't a CV be enough? While yes, most office positions do only ask for a CV, keep in mind that you'll be competing against other people directly. This means that every point you've got on the competition looks great. You're also presenting less as an employee and more as a business partner, and what kind of business partner doesn't have a website?

The first question you should be asking yourself is "Do I have any close contacts?" Chances are, if you've been working in the IT industry, you know quite a few people with websites. In fact, with most IT professionals, this might even be the bulk of people you know. If this is the case, then great, you've got some potential clients right there. Reach out to all of these people one by one and check if they've been having issues with finding a cybersecurity professional.

If any say yes, then great! You've got your first gig, so make sure to completely nail it. If you do so, then they'll be sure to recommend you to their friends. This is the most important part of freelancing—making a network of useful contacts that can be clients whenever you come into a pinch. Make sure that all of your past employers/clients know what you're working as right now, and tell them to recommend you if anyone they know is having cybersecurity issues.

This is great because it:

1. Builds your reputation. You will become much more well-known in your field if even people that don't dabble in cybersecurity know your name. Furthermore, having people that are ready to vouch for your quality is an excellent sign for future clients.

2. It builds a consistent clientele. After you've gotten a few successful gigs, chances are, clients will start flowing in by themselves. Word of mouth spreads fast in tech circles, and quality cybersecurity professionals are very few.

So, what if your past clients don't give you any gigs? Or they simply aren't eager enough to recommend you to their acquaintances? In that case, go over to social media, and job sites like Indeed.

There are countless postings for remote/freelance cybersecurity experts and ethical hackers on these sites. Make sure that you're using these to their fullest potential. Put "ethical hacker," "penetration tester," or "cybersecurity expert" into your bio. Other than that, make sure you're using Linkedin, as it's very popular among recruitment managers, and sometimes even having a well-made profile is enough to get you a few potential clients.

Indeed is generally best for long-term remote positions, though it isn't too bad for freelance ones either. Keep in mind that Indeed is a numbers game. A lot of the listings are fake or outdated, so make sure you're applying to tons.

Now, if none of these have worked, then it's time to turn to an aggregate site. This would be a site like UpWork or Freelancer, which are sites designed to promote bidding among freelancers for jobs.

Generally, I'd advise against using these sites, as they tend to give out lower rates than individually found clients would. On the other hand, if you've got a good portfolio of experience, you'll soon move past the beginner-level jobs (of which there are many) and move onto jobs that are actually well paid.

I Have No Experience, What Do I Do?

If you've just gotten into the world of ethical hacking and have no experience whatsoever to speak of, do not despair. After all, you have a solid foundation of knowledge, and a drive to succeed!

In this case, I'd advise to have someone make your website for you. Chances are, you either don't know enough to do it yourself, or would lose yourself to options paralysis. If you feel like you know enough and are decisive enough to do it well, then by all means do it yourself. On the other hand, hiring a professional is always a good idea.

After you're done with that, I suggest having a few portfolio pieces. They can be practice work you did in university, or just stuff you did to mess around for fun, but the important part is for it to be *something* you can display to prospective clients.

At that point, go to one of the freelance aggregate sites like UpWork or Freelancer (out of these two, I'd recommend UpWork as it seems more professional) and start hunting for gigs. Don't be afraid if you're only getting accepted for low-paying gigs, as these sites are notoriously built on reputation and experience. Make sure that you're always moving up. Every one of your clients should be better-paying than your last one.

After you've amassed a considerable amount of experience on one of these sites, come back here and apply the advice in the "I have experience, now what?" section.

Bounties

In either case (with experience or not), bounties are a solid, if extremely difficult, way to earn money. Bounties are mainly geared towards those with experience, but there have been cases where they've been obtained by those with less experience.

A bounty is when a company decides it wants its cybersecurity to be tested, and then they let anyone have a go at it. If any white hat succeeds at cracking a company's defenses, then they get what is known as a "bounty." So, in essence, you'd be pretending to be a malicious cracker that is trying to get into the company's systems, and if you succeed, then you get money. Sounds good, doesn't it?

The thing with bounties, however, is that for less proficient hackers, they're often more hassle than it's worth. After all, those that are worth doing will usually be taken by the top 5% of hackers worldwide, rather than the average joe of the ethical hacking world.

Chapter 4: The Three Hats

Wait, hats? Yes, weirdly enough, out of all the things in the world, hackers are actually separated by hats. Now, as we've already explored, just because someone is a hacker, it doesn't mean they're involved in illegal activity or anything of the like. You'll find that most people, online or otherwise, refer to hackers under one of three labels. These are white, grey, and black hat. The grey hat is sometimes considered a specific subset of black. These are terms which were created in order to define different hackers based on what they do, and we touched on each briefly in the intro.

On a similar note, it can be quite hard to define "hacker," as the term's technical use is rather different from the way that it is used in most of pop culture. With that being said, we can definitely say that a hacker is someone that uses a hole in a digital system to find ways to exploit and receive personal gain from it. In the case of white hat hackers, this gain would either be money provided by the firm that hired them, or the satisfaction of knowing they did something good.

So, what exactly *are* the three hats of hackers and what do they do?

Black Hats

Black hat hackers, mostly referred to as "black hats," are those hackers that are most often featured in pop culture, TV shows, and movies. This is the type of hacker you think of when you hear the word hacker. Black hat hackers are those that will break the law, as well as break into a computer's security in order to pursue a selfish agenda. This can be something ranging from simply stealing credit card numbers to stealing whole identities off of people.

In other cases, this is simply done out of malice, so a black hat hacker might make a botnet purely for the sake of DDOS-ing the websites that they aren't particularly fond of.

Black hats not only fit the stereotype that hackers are criminals, but are also the reason for its existence. They are basically the PC equivalent of highly trained robbers. It's not hard to see why other hacker groups generally aren't very fond of black hats, as they besmirch the others' names.

Black hats are often those that find zero day vulnerabilities in a site's or company's security, and then sell it to other organizations, or simply use it for their own selfish agendas instead.

Zero Day Vulnerability?

A zero-day is a flaw in a given piece of either hardware, software, or firmware which isn't known to any of the parties which would otherwise be tasked with patching up said flaw. The term itself can refer either to the vulnerability in itself, or alternatively, an attack which gives 0 days between discovering the vulnerability and attacking. When a zero day vulnerability is made known to the public, then it will be known as an n-day or one-day vulnerability, both of which are equally dangerous.

Usually, when a flaw like this is detected, then the person that detected it will bring said flaw to the company whose software is flawed. Occasionally, they'll announce the flaw publicly in case they can't reach the company itself. This is usually done in the interest of patching up that hole.

Given some time, the company which made the program can usually fix it and distribute the patch for it. Sometimes, this will mean delaying the product a bit, but after all, is it not worth it to do that if it means it saves the company a lot of money? Even if the vulnerability is made public, it can often take black hats a while to actually become able to exploit it. In these scenarios, it's pretty much a race between the black hats and white hats.

On the other hand, sometimes it is a black hat that first discovers the vulnerability. If it isn't known in advance, then the white hats at the company won't have any idea that the exploit even exists before it is used against them. Usually, these companies will employ ethical hackers to try to find such zero-day vulnerabilities, so they can be fixed up before their product reaches the market.

Security researchers operate together with information vendors who will often agree to not share any zero-day vulnerability information until they're allowed. For example, Google's own Project Zero suggests that, if you should find a vulnerability as a person not employed by the company, you should wait at least 90 days before disclosing the vulnerability to the public. On the other hand, if the vulnerability is something really critical, then Google suggests that you should wait only about 7 days to see if the company will close up the gaping hole they accidentally left open. On the other hand, if the vulnerability is already being exploited, then fire away!

Black Hat Hacker Example

Much like in the opening scenes of a movie starring Daniel Craig, all the way back in 1994, Vladimir Levin used his laptop in his St. Petersburg apartment in order to commit the first internet bank heist in history.

He transferred $10 million from accounts of various Citibank clients to a variety of accounts he owned around the world. Fortunately, this heist didn't go all that well for Levin. He was captured and imprisoned only three years later. Of the $10 million that he stole, only $400,000 was never found. The way Levin did this was actually incredibly simple. He simply hacked into clients' calls, noted their account information, then just went and gave their money to himself.

White Hats

Hey, this is us! White hat hackers, also often referred to as ethical hackers, are the direct opposite of black hat hackers. They're also experts at compromising computer security systems, so much so that many of them used to be black hats in the past, and reformed. These are the hackers which could be black hats, but rather choose to use their skills and knowledge for good, and for ethical purposes rather than their own selfish motivations (although you could argue that the pursuit of good is selfish in and of itself).

Most white hats are employed by companies in order to try and "simulate" a black hat, so they will try to break into an organization's security systems as best they could. The organization then authorizes the white hat hackers to use their knowledge of security systems in order to compromise the whole organization. Does this sound like something a black hat would do? Precisely. They need to simulate exactly what a black hat hacker would do, so that they can know whether or not they'll be able to stop them before they've dealt significant damage to the company. The attacks of a white hat hacker are generally used in order to enhance the organization's defenses against cyberattacks. Usually, these two things will be done by the same people, however, some companies will have white hat hackers and cybersecurity professionals separate.

The method of impersonating a black hat hacker to gain access to a company's confidential files in order to help them with their system is known as penetration testing.

You'll find that white hat hackers that find vulnerabilities in securities would rather disclose the same to the developer of the program, rather than fulfilling their own selfish desires.

If you accidentally find a vulnerability as an ethical hacker, it is your moral obligation to report it to the developer. With this, you're allowing them to patch their product before a black hat hacker can get to it and ruin it entirely.

It's also worth noting that, like we mentioned before, some organizations pay bounties even for anonymous white hats that are good enough to get into their system. By doing this, they ensure that they're safe from any black hats that might've infiltrated their ranks as white hats, as well as reaching a wider audience.

White Hat Hacker Example

Kevin Mitnick is pretty much the face of the ethical hacking movement these days, however, that wasn't always the case. In fact, many speculate that the reason for his fame, as well as his skills, is due to the fact that his hat wasn't always precisely the whitest of them all.

26 years ago, in 1995, the police force caught Mitnick in a high-profile arrest. He had been committing a spree of hacking activities that lasted for over 2 years. All of it was entirely illegal. Some of his exploits were truly massive. For example, during one of his escapades, he broke into the security systems of the Digital Equipment Corp. Once he was in, he decided to copy everything that was there, and copy he did.

After serving his jail sentence, he got some supervised release time, but before his time was even done, Mitnick had gone back to his old ways. In fact, before his punishment was served, he got entry into the Pacific Bell voicemail computers. It is thought that he got into several other places illegally, using methods like intercepting passwords, though this was never actually confirmed.

He got a solid 46 months for that, and 22 on top of that because he violated the time where he was supposed to be in supervised release. This was what finally marked the end of his career as a black hat hacker.

After serving his sentence, back in 2000, Mitnick decided he'd become a white hat hacker. He elected to become a paid consultant, and consult he did. Fortune 500 companies and even the FBI flocked to Mitnick for help. After all, he had a trove of talents and knowledge to share. There have been tons of people flocking to him over the years in order to learn from the experience he had. The knowledge and ideas that he possessed were then transitioned into his highly popular public speaking and writing work.

Mitnick has even taught classes himself, leading social engineering classes to possess the same knowledge that he used to. These were vital skills that we still need today. Even today, Mitnick is busy doing penetration tests, though now it's for some of the world's most successful and powerful companies.

Gray Hats

Nothing in life is black or white. Moving on, that unfunny joke is actually quite reflective of hacking. In fact, much like in life, there's always a grey area between white and black in the world of hacking.

As you should have guessed, a grey hat hacker sits in the awkward spot between a black hat hacker and a white hat. The grey hat hacker isn't exactly working for their own personal gain, or even just to do damage, but they do sometimes commit crimes, and do things that others might deem unethical. At other times, they're those that do something that's illegal, but at the same time, ethical.

Let's try to explain this. A black hat hacker is the kind of person that will get into a computer system without getting permission from anyone, and then proceed to steal the data that is inside it in order to achieve some kind of personal gain, or in order to vandalize the system. A white hat would ask for permission, they would test the system's security only after receiving it, and they wouldn't do anything with that other than inform the organization about the vulnerability, as well as how to fix it.

On the other hand, a grey hat hacker wouldn't do any of these things most of the time. While they didn't do it for malicious purposes, they still broke into a system without permission. At one end of the spectrum, a grey hat hacker would simply do this for fun, at which point they're much closer to black hat than white hat. On the other hand, they might have also done it to help the organization, even without permission, in which case they'd be much closer to white hat.

In case a grey hat hacker discovers a gaping security hole, it's hard to guess what they'd do. Anything between simply doing nothing, to alerting the company directly, would be possible. On the other hand, the "average" response, I'd reckon, is revealing the flaw publicly so that the company will have the time to fix it, but also not bothering enough to contact them directly.

It's worth noting that all of these things fall into the water if this is done for personal gain. In that case, this falls into black hat behavior. Even if the public disclosure later causes chaos (because a black hat found it) or helps the company (because a white hat found it), that doesn't change anything for the grey hat.

Grey Hat Hacker Example

In August of 2013, Khalil Shreateh was an unemployed computer security expert. He decided he'd hack the Facebook page of Mark Zuckerberg. The, Mark Zuckerberg. Surprisingly, he was successful. Facebook's CEO was forced to face something that Khalil had been telling them about for quite a while.

The truth was that Khalil had discovered a bug that allowed people to post to pretty much anyone's page without their consent. He tried, with no avail, to inform Facebook of this. After getting told repeatedly that this was not a bug, Khalil took the matter into his own hands.

Khalil hacked into the CEO's page and pointed out how much of an issue this bug could be. After all, malicious spammers could use it for a variety of things, and that's only scratching the surface of potential abuses that this could have.

After this happened, Facebook finally decided to correct this issue, which could have caused them millions in losses. Unfortunately, Khalil didn't get any compensation for his work from Facebook's White Hat program, which was due to him needing to violate their policies to find the issue.

As well as knowing what the terms mean, it is important to note that people can be multiple hats, and that the terms can be used for behavior, rather than just people. For example, someone could both do penetration testing for one company, while also hacking into another maliciously. This would make them both a black and a white hat hacker.

Behavior is much easier to understand when it's explained. Basically, ask yourself the question, "If a person did this every day, which kind of hacker would they be considered?" And you've got your answer as to what kind of hacker they are.

Chapter 5: Ethical Hacking Explained

When it comes to security, being a hacker is one of the most overused terms. It appears everywhere, and even the entertainment industry and many authors use it often in their films, books, TV shows, and other media forms. Because of this, the word "hacker" is mostly viewed as a bad profession and always connected to shady or real criminal activities. So, when people hear that someone is involved in hacking, they immediately see that person as somebody who doesn't have good intentions. They are mostly represented as "operators from the shadow", even antisocial. On the other hand, they are also viewed as a social activist. This label became especially popular after a few affairs such as WikiLeaks. Many hackers were involved in obtaining many important documents from governments, politicians, and corporations that showed information that was very different from that given to the public. Also, organized groups such as Anonymous or Lizard Squad had a huge influence on the perception of hackers in recent years.

The Evolution of Hacking

Initially, hacking appeared out of curiosity. Technology enthusiasts wanted to know how systems worked and what they could do with them. Today, we also have many of those who like to experiment, customize, and improve original designs. In the early 1970s, hackers were actually people who could have been found in their houses taking apart radios, early computers, and other devices of that era and figuring out how they worked. With the progress of technology, this kind of individuals advanced along with it. Later, in the 1980s when the PC was the highest achievement of technology, hackers moved to that environment and even started to engage in more suspicious activities, often malicious. The reason for this was also the fact that the attacks could impact more systems since more and more people had PCs. When the Internet became a thing in the 1990s, all of the systems connected to it became interconnected, too. The result was obvious – curiosity mixed with bad intentions was now available worldwide and since it was easier to hack different computer systems, more and more hackers appeared.

At the beginning of the 21st century, computers stopped being the only devices that could be hacked. In the meantime, we acquired other technologies such as smartphones, Bluetooth devices, tablets, and many other things that hackers could use as their targets. It is very simple. Not only does technology evolve, hackers do, too. So, if the system is complicated, the hacker's attack is going to be harder to escape. And when the Internet started to be a part of everything that we do, different types of data became easier to access. The first hackers' internet attacks in the 1990s were usually connected to website defacements and many of these cyberspace attacks ended up being pranks, sometimes funny and interesting, but sometimes they ended up being very serious, even criminal activities. More aggressive attacks started to occur such as hacking websites of different governments, or something that you are probably more familiar with – hacking of film websites that resulted in many pirate websites that are active even today.

As we already mentioned, from the beginning of the 2000s cyberspace attacks became more frequent and more malicious. Additionally, these attacks were progressing fast. At the time, there were already hacking activities classified as advances. Many of these hackers had criminal motives and even though we can't say that there is a standard classification for them, we will set them in several categories:

- There were hackers who used their skills to manipulate stock prices which caused many financial complications

- Some of them hacked people's personal data, thus they were stealing identities

- One of the most frequent hacker attacks was connected to credit card theft or cyberspace vandalism

- Also, as we mentioned before, piracy was quite common and at some point even popular

- The last but not the least type of hacking attack that was usually from the early 2000s was a denial of service and service attacks.

As you know, over the last few decades, most financial transactions have been made online, which is a tempting field for crooks. But not only that, the openness of mobile phones, laptops, tablets, and similar devices that we use daily also increased the space and how every kind of information can be stolen. An increasing number of internet users, users of different gadgets, and similar software products that connect people and their devices in multiple ways increased the number of those who have an interest in obtaining some part of it.

All of these mischievous activities over the years resulted in new laws in almost every country in the world. These laws emerged from the need to gain control over cyberspace criminal activities. Although the number of website hackings became lower, organized cybercrime increased.

Examples: Mischief or Criminal?

Hacking is by no means a phenomenon that appeared overnight. It existed in different forms and evolved all the way from the 1960s. However, in the beginning, it was never addressed as a criminal activity. We will view a few cases that will give you a closer look at some of the attacks, and generic examples that gradually changed that picture.

One of the most famous hacking groups in the world called the "Anonymous" appeared in 2003. They were responsible for a series of attacks on government websites and other networks. They also hacked many news agencies and other organizations. These multiple successful intrusions ranked them among one of the most active cyber organized groups ever. The interesting thing is that they are still active and committed to attacking high-profiled targets.

During the mid-2000s, a new computer virus was discovered. The name of this virus was Stuxnet and it had a specific design that attacked only systems that had any kind of connection with the production of uranium. The unique feature of this program was the fact that it ignored other systems, and it attacked only if the requirements mentioned above were met.

Another interesting case is the case of a young Russian hacker named Kristina Vladimirovna Scechinskaya who was involved in a plot to defraud some of the biggest banks in Great Britain and the United States. The whole thing started in 2009 when she used the famous "Trojan horse" virus to open thousands of accounts while attacking others. The total amount of the money that she succeeded in stealing in the scam was 3 billion dollars. She was called the world's sexiest hacker, which helped with breaking the stereotype of hackers being antisocial beings living in the basement and so forth.

All of these cases are some of the most famous high-profile hacking incidents that happened, even though maybe some of them didn't gain that much media coverage. In fact, many of the cybercriminal cases that appear in the news stay unresolved, but many others had a huge impact on different industries but never make it to the breaking news or ended up persecuted for cybercrime.

Now that we have reviewed some concrete incidents, we will name some of the other activities that are considered to be cybercrimes. We will call them generic examples, but keep in mind that these are not the only ones. Many other forms can be viewed as illegal.

- Gaining access to any services or resources that you don't have permission for. This is mostly referred to as stealing usernames and passwords. There are some cases in which obtaining this information without permission is considered a cybercrime even if you don't use them or they are the accounts of friends or family members.

- There is a form of digital trespassing called Network intrusions that is also considered to be a cybercrime. In essence, just like ordinary trespassing, this means that you went someplace without permission to enter (or in this case access). So in the case where someone acquires access to a system or group of systems without authorization we can say that the person violated the network, thus committed cybercrime. Still, some network intrusions can happen without using hacker tools. Sometimes logging into guest accounts without previous authorization can be viewed as cybercrime.

- One of the most complex, yet one of the simplest forms of hacking is by going after the most vulnerable element in the system – humans. This form of cybercrime is known as social engineering, and we say that it can be simply because the person may be a far more accessible component of the system than any other, and it is easier to interact with. However, people can give cues that are difficult to understand whether they are spoken or not, which makes it hard for the hacker to get the information that they need.

- The issue of posting or transmitting illegal materials became difficult to deal with in general, especially in the last decade. Social media gained much attention and many other services that are internet-related increased in usage and popularity. This enabled many illegal materials to go from one place to another in the shortest time possible, thus it can spread very fast

- Fraud is also a thing that often happens, especially on the Internet, and it is also considered to be a cybercrime. Just like the original term, fraud in cyberspace also means that a party or parties were deceived typically for the purpose of financial gain or causing damage.

What Does it Mean to be an Ethical Hacker?

All of the things that we previously mentioned in this chapter referred to hackers in general. However, the real goal is to learn how to be an ethical hacker and explore the skills that one should have.

Ethical hackers are people employed usually by organizations to test their security. They usually work through direct employment or through temporary contracts. The key is that they use the same skills as all other hackers, but there is one big difference- they have permission to attack the system directly from the system's owner. Additionally, being an ethical hacker means that you reveal the weaknesses of the system you evaluated (because every system in the world has them) only to the owner and to no one else. Furthermore, organizations or individuals that hire ethical hackers use very strict contracts that specify which parts of the system are authorized for an attack and which are off-limits. The role of an ethical hacker also depends on the job that he or she is entitled to, thus the needs of the employer. Nowadays, some organizations have teams that are permanent staff members and their job is to perform ethical hacking activities.

Hackers can be divided into 5 categories. Keep in mind that this categorization may vary, but we can say that these are the most common ones:

- The first category is also known as "Script Kiddies". These hackers usually don't have any training or they do, but very limited. They know how to use only some of the basic hacking tools and techniques and since they are not skillful enough, it can happen that sometimes even they don't fully understand their doings or the consequences that their work might have.

- The second category involves hackers known as "White Hat hackers". They attack the computer system, but they are the good guys which means that they cause no harm to their work. These kinds of hackers are most frequently ethical hackers, but they can be pen-testers too.

- "Grey Hat hackers" are the third hacker category. As their name suggests, they are in between being good and bad but their final decision is to choose the good side. Still, these kinds of hackers have difficulties gaining trust since they can act suspicious.

- The fourth category that we will mention in this section is labeled as the "Black Hat hackers". This category refers to the hackers that we mentioned before in this chapter. These people usually work on the "other side" of the law and they are usually connected to criminal activities.

- Last but not least are the "Suicide hackers". They are called this because their goal is to prove the point, and that is why they want to knock out their target. These hackers don't worry about being caught because their purpose is not to hide but to prove, so they are easier to find.

Responsibilities of an Ethical Hacker

The most important thing that an ethical hacker should learn and never forget is that he or she always needs to have permission for any kind of system attack. The ethical code that you need to implement in every task as an ethical hacker says that no network or system should be tested or targeted if you don't own it or if you don't own permission for it. Otherwise, you can be seen as guilty for multiple crimes that can happen in the meantime. Firstly, that can harm your career, and secondly, if it's something very serious, it can even threaten your freedom, too.

The smartest thing to do is to have a contract from your employer close at the time of testing or attacking the required target. The contract represents a written authorization, but you have to keep in mind that you are allowed to examine only the parts of the system specified in that contract. So, if your employer wants to give you permission to hack additional parts of the system or to remove authorization for some, he should alter the contract first, and you shouldn't operate further until you get the new permit. Note that the only thing that distinguishes an ethical hacker from the cybercriminal is the contract. Therefore, you should always pay special attention to the verbiage that deals with privacy and confidentiality issues because it often happens that you come across intimate information of your client whether business or personal.

That is one more reason why your contract should include to whom you can talk about the things you found while examining the system and who is forbidden to hear any updates from you. In general, clients usually want to be the only people who know everything you eventually find out.

An organization known as EC Council (International Council of Electronic Commerce Consultants) is one of the most important organizations when it comes to regulation of these issues. According to them, an ethical hacker has to keep private any kind of information acquired during work and treat it as confidential. This is especially pointed out for client's personal information, which means that you are not allowed to transfer, give, sell, collect, or do something similar with any of the client's information such as Social Security number, email address, home address, unique identifier, name, and so forth. The only way you can give this kind of information to a third party is to have written consent from your employer (client).

Even though some might argue about the distinctions of hackers and ethical hackers, the division is quite straightforward-hackers are separated by their intentions. This means that those who intend to do harm and use their skills to access data without permission are labeled as black hats, while those who work with their client's consent are considered to be white hat hackers.

Naming these two categories "the bad one" and "the good one" can be controversial, so we will try to adhere to these expressions in the following manner:

- Black hats typically work outside the law which means that they don't have authorization from the person referred to as "the client" to consent to their activities.

- Contrarily, white hats do have authorization and consent from the person referred to as "client" and they even keep the information they have between the client and white hats alone.

- Gray hats, on the other hand, cross into both of these territories and they use both kinds of actions at different periods.

Hacktivists are a category of hackers that we haven't mentioned before. They belong to the movement known as Hacktivism which refers to actions that hackers use to impact the general public by promoting a certain political agenda. So far, hacktivists have been involved with agencies, big corporations, and governments.

Ethics and Code of Conduct for Hackers

Like every other profession, even hacking has its Code of Conduct that sets rules which can help clients (individuals or organizations) to evaluate if the person that deals with their networks and computer systems, in general, is trustworthy. The organization that has conducted this Code was already mentioned in the previous sections and it is known as EC-Council. Obtaining a CEH credential from the EC-Council means that you fully understand the expectations that you need to abide by. We have provided some parts of the code, so make sure you read it and familiarize yourself with it.

- Information that you gain during your professional work should be kept confidential and private (especially personal information)

- Unless you have your client's consent, you can't give, transfer, or sell the client's home address, name, or other uniquely identifying information.

- You have to protect the intellectual property, yours and that of others, by using skills that you acquired on your own so that all of the benefits go to its original creator.

- Be sure to disclose to the authorized personnel any danger that you suspect can come from the Internet community, electronic transactions, or other hardware and software indicator.

- Make sure that the services you provide are in the area of your expertise, thus you work honestly while being aware of any potential limitations that might be a consequence of your education or experience.

- You should work only on projects that you are qualified for and do jobs that match your skills in terms of training, education, and work experience.

- You mustn't knowingly use any software obtained illegally or retained unethically.

- You can't participate in any financial practices that can be viewed as deceptive such as double billing, bribery, and so on.

- Make sure that you use the client's property properly, without crossing the limits set on your contract.

- You should disclose a potential conflict of interest to all parties concerned, especially if that conflict can't be avoided.

- Make sure that you provide good management for the entire project that you are working on including activities for promotion and risk disclosure.

Chapter 6: How to Scan Your System

There are several ways to scan your computer. However, it is important to understand that different scans pursue a different type of data, thus achieve different results. That is why you should look into the scan more carefully before you go into that kind of process. Scans, in general, share a similar theme which is based on the premise that its purpose is to collect information about one or more hosts. Still, if you dig deeper, you will see that some differences emerge along the way. Every scan gives different feedback on the type of data it gains, therefore, each one is valuable in its own way. To avoid complicating things we will use simple categorization and say that there are three categories and that they all have their specific characteristics.

Port Scan

The first category that we will mention is called the port scan. This is a process in which packets or messages are carefully sent to the computer that you are targeting. The intention of this scan is data gathering and these probes are most frequently connected to the number of ports or those types that have less or equal to 1024 ones. If this technique is applied carefully, there are many things that you can learn about the possibilities that a system that you are scanning has to offer to the whole network. You can even find differences between systems such as controllers of domains, web servers, mail servers, and so on, during the process.

One of the most commonly used port scanners is known as Fyodor's map. Port scanning is one of the most used types of scanning and it often happens that other people assume that you talk about port scanning just by mentioning the "scan" term.

Network Scan

Network scan is the second category of scanning that we'll mention. It is designed specifically to find all hosts that are "live" on a certain network which means that this scan will find all of the hosts that are running through the system at the time. It will identify which systems might be targeted or find hosts that can scan further. These kinds of scans are known as ping sweeps too, and they can scan the IPs' range very fast and then establish if the address had a host that is powered-on attached to it. The most common example of a network scan is Angry IP, but there are many others used to achieve the same goal.

Vulnerability Scan

The third category is known as vulnerability scan and it is used to find all of the weaknesses of the targeted system. The most common reason to use this kind of scan is if the client wants proactive measures, especially if there is a doubt that someone might attack it. The goal of those who want a vulnerability scan is to intentionally grasp the situation about potential problems and act on them as fast as possible. Classic vulnerability scans gain information about access points, hosts, ports (especially the opened ones); it analyzes the response of all services, generates reports, and as a very important feature it classifies threats if there are any. They are popular among large corporations because they can be used to find easy access to the system. The two most frequently used vulnerability scanners are Rapid7 Nexpose and Tenable Nessus. Additionally, there are many specialized scanners on the market, and the most famous ones are Nikto, Burp Suite, WebInspect, and so forth.

To avoid potential misunderstandings that can appear before an ethical hacker, you should know the difference between penetration testing and vulnerability. First of all, vulnerability scan has the purpose of finding out the weaknesses that a host or a network has, but it doesn't exploit the weak points it finds. On the other hand, penetration tests go a step further and not only can find the same weaknesses but uses them, intending to find out how far an attacker could go if they find them, too.

You probably wonder what kind of information a penetration test provides. The answer can't be simple; still, some general assumptions can be made. When you scan a system, it is highly probable that you will encounter many different data sets. We can list them as follows to make it easier:

- Network's live hosts

- Architecture of the system

- Opened and closed ports and information that the host

has on the operating system (or more systems)

- Running processes on the host system

- Type of system's weaknesses and their level

- Patches that the target system has

- Information on firewalls' presence

- Routers and their addresses along with other information

When you take a closer look, it is clear why many people define scanning as a type of intelligence-gathering process that can be used by real attackers. If you are creative and skillful enough you can perform a successful scan. However, if you hit a roadblock while scanning, your skills have to come in and you have to see what your next move will be. Keep in mind that once you gather information, it will take some time to analyze it, and that also depends on how good you are at reading the results that the scan gave you. The more knowledge you have, the easier it will be to decipher results.

Live Systems Check

Let's begin with finding the targets that you'd probe and investigate. Keep in mind that even though you gained information about the range of IP or IPs that are owned by your client (individual or organization), it doesn't mean that each of those IP addresses will have a host that is connected to it. The first thing you need to do if you want to have meaningful progress is to find which "pulses" are real and which aren't, thus which IPs have hosts. The question is, how will you check if there are live systems in the environment that you target? The answer is actually simple. There are many ways to do that. Still, the ones that are most commonly used are port scanning, war dialing, pinging and wardriving. Each of these techniques has its own value since they all provide certain information that is unique to their designs. Once you learn more about them, you will understand how they work and what differences they have and it will be easier to implement the one you need more for a penetration test.

War Dialing

War dialing is an old but useful way to scan the system. It was practically unchanged from the 1980s and the reason why it's still used is because it has proven to be one of the most reliable and useful tools for information gathering. When it comes to practice, this technique is quite straightforward in comparison to other scanning forms. War dialing works on the principle of dialing a block of different phone numbers while using modems that are considered to be standard. Once the scan dials the numbers, it can determine the locations of the systems that also have their modem attached and that are accepting connections. At first glance it may seem that this is an old-fashioned mechanism, however, it is more than useful on multiple levels.

The main one is the fact that modems are still widely used since they are affordable and have good phone lines that are basically everywhere.

One of the reasons why modems are still in usage is that they serve as a backup to the existing technologies. So if other connectivity options fail, lines provided by phones will be available to prevent major outages. For corporations, it is a good deal because it is affordable and it gives some type of security in case something really big happens.

So, the question that follows is what happens when you find a modem. Firstly, you need to be familiarized with the devices that are commonly connected to modems nowadays. For example, PBXs (Private Branch Exchanges) frequently have non-digital modes attached to them. These kinds of modems are good for different kinds of mischief from an attacker. However, some modems have firewalls attached to them, or fax machines, routers, and so on. So when attackers gain access through a firewall, the environment of the device won't be protected for long. You should be mindful of pivot points when accessing the system. Pivot points are systems that are compromised and then used to attack other systems, making their environment unsafe. Over the years, many programs have been created as war dialing programs. The best-known ones are:

Tone Loc, which is a program based on looking for dial tones by dialing random numbers that are within an attacker's range. This program can also search for the carrier frequency of a modem. It takes inputs with area codes and number ranges that an attacker wants to dial.

PhoneSweep from Niksun, which is a program that represents one of the few options that are commercially available on the market.

THC-SCAN ADOS, which is a program based on dialing phone numbers using modems and looks for a carrier frequency from that modem.

Ping

Another commonly used tool for scanning is called ping. Ping is used to determine the connectivity of a network by establishing if the remote host is located up or down. Although it is a quite simple feature, it is still highly efficient for the initial process of scanning. Ping is based on ICMP (Internet Control Message Protocol) messages and that is why this kind of scanning is sometimes called an ICMP scan. It works simply. One system sends an echo (in this case an ICMP echo) to another system and if it's alive, it will reply by sending another ICMP echo as a response. When the initial system receives this reply, it confirms that the target is live or up.

Ping tells you not only if the target is alive, but it also gains information on the speed of target packets and TTL (time to live) data. If you want to use ping in Windows, you should just enter the following prompt command: ping or ping. The Linux versions use the same command, but the command will constantly ping the target unless you press ctrl+c to stop the process.

Even though you can use ping to access hostnames and IP addresses, it is recommended that you ping by IP address rather than hostname technique first because inactive hostname might mean that there is a DNS issue rather than an unavailable system. Keep in mind that if you have a system to ping, you ping it, and don't receive a response although you know that the targeted system is working, the targeted system may have a disabled ping service. If that is true, you won't receive any response from that type of system at all.

Ports and Checking Their Status

When you locate the network's live systems, the next step is to take a look at the hosts once again. The goal is to determine whether they have any open ports or not. Generally speaking, what you are doing is zooming in on every live host that you've previously found and examining the ports to establish if any of them are opened. However, in this phase, you can only see if there are opened or closed ports, but you can't do anything about it since that advanced feature comes in some more advanced sections. Remember that knowing the ports and port scans is one of the essential skills for ethical hacking and when you examine different types of port scans that exist, you will know in which situations you'll prefer one over another. Be mindful of details because, at the end of the day, studying is the best way to improve your skills.

Chapter 7: Penetration Testing

Penetration testing, also known as pen testing, is one of the main activities ethical hackers do. A penetration test is also called a white hat attack due to the fact that it is done by a white hat hacker for the purpose of helping out a system's owner. It is a process of finding vulnerabilities in applications, networks, and systems that could potentially be exploited by malicious users that are trying to get into the system. The process can be executed manually, but it can also be automated through the use of other applications. No matter how you do it, the goal of the process always stays the same. First, you gather as much information as possible about the target before starting the test. This boils down to finding entry points and attempting to break into the system, as well as collecting the findings into one document.

No matter how you approach the process, its goal always remains the same: to find weaknesses in the security of a system. This is mostly done digitally, but can also be done in the physical part of computer security. As you know, there are methods of hacking that involve using the staff in order to get into the system. Penetration testing can be used to test how much employees are aware of security policies, as well as how quickly an organization can recognize a threat.

After the ethical hacker has identified the exploitable weaknesses of a system, they notify the IT and network system managers of the organization. Based on this, these experts can take measures that will help out with the security of their systems, as well as allocate the necessary resources for this.

The Purpose of Penetration Testing

The main goal of a penetration test is finding out if the system has any vulnerabilities that could be abused to destabilize the system's security, as well as see if the security complies with the standard and test how well the employees of a company know the security issues. This is done in order to determine how the organization would be affected by a potential break in, as well as how the vulnerabilities can be fixed.

This can also lead to discovering the faults in the security policies of a company. Some companies, for example, have many policies regarding the detection and prevention of a hacking attack, but have none regarding how to expel the hacker.

Cloud Pen Testing Responsibilities

In some networks you might find different combinations of on-premises systems and cloud systems. This means that the pen testing responsibilities tend to vary between different networks.

We have already mentioned how important reports are in penetration testing. They will usually give the company a lot of helpful insight into their security system and help them prioritize the improvements to the security system they had planned. These reports give app developers the incentive to create more secure applications. By understanding how hackers get into their applications, the developers can educate them further on how to make their future projects more secure so that similar vulnerabilities do not pop up ever again.

How Often Should You Perform Penetration Tests?

Usually, companies do this on a regular basis. This is typically done once a year. The more often they do penetration testing, the more efficient the work of the security and IT management gets. On top of the regularly executed penetration tests, companies also do them when:

- The company adds a new infrastructure or application to their system

- The company makes large modifications to their system

- The company adds new offices in a different location

- The company adds new security patches

- The company modifies its security policies

You should realize, however, that penetration testing doesn't go the same for every company. How pen testing goes depends on many factors like:

- How large is the company? The larger the presence of a company, the higher the chance of the company being under attack by a hacker, as they have more attack approaches and juicier pay-offs.

- How much money can the company give for penetration testing? Smaller companies cannot always afford to do them on a yearly basis due to the fact that the process can cost quite a bit of money. Only the more lucrative companies to it on a yearly basis, while the smaller ones do it once every two years.

- What does the law say? In some industries, there are laws that require companies to do security tasks.

- Some companies have their infrastructures in the cloud. Sometimes these companies cannot run their own penetration tests and the responsibility falls onto the provider himself.

Every company has different needs when it comes to penetration testing. This is why white hat hackers need to be very flexible when it comes to penetration testing, as their efforts will be more efficient if the penetration testing they do is tailored to the company they are working for. After every penetration test, it is recommended to run several more follow-up tests to make sure that the results are noted in the penetration tests that are yet to come.

Penetration Testing Tools

Penetration testing can be automated due to the number of tools that are available today. These tools are usually used by pen testers in order to quickly scan the system for common vulnerabilities. They are used to scan code to find malicious parts which can be used to breach the system. They find vulnerabilities in the system by examining the encryption techniques and hard-coded values.

Penetration Test Strategies

Whenever a white hat hacker is approaching a penetration test, they should always define the scope in which they will operate. This usually tells the tester which parts of the system they should approach, as well as which tools and techniques should be used while working. This helps allocate resources and manpower more efficiently while doing a penetration test.

If a penetration tester that was hired by the company gains access to the system because they found a password of an employee in plain sight, this tells the security team that the security practices of the employee are lacking and show where improvements need to be made.

There are many strategies that penetration testers use relatively often:

- Targeted testing

The company's IT team is usually in charge of targeted testing. They work in tandem with the penetration testers in order to do this. This approach is sometimes referred to as the "lights turned on" approach due to the fact that everyone has access to the results and execution of this test.

- External testing

External testing is executed in order to find weaknesses in the parts of the system that are visible from the exterior. This includes firewalls, web servers, email servers, and domain names. The objective of this kind of penetration test is to find out if that part of the system can be used to access the deeper parts of the system and how far the hacker can get during that attack.

- Internal testing

An attack performed during internal testing starts from behind the firewall and is done by a user that has standard access privileges. This is usually done in order to see what extent of damage can be done by an employee of the company that has malicious intents.

- Blind Testing

Blind testing has this name because the information available to the tester is greatly limited due to the fact that it is made to emulate what kind of path a real attacker would take in a quick job. These testers are used to emulate an actual all-out attack that a malicious individual from outside the company would commit and are given almost nothing other than the name of the company that is hiring them. This kind of test can take quite a bit of time due to the time the hacker needs to find where they can access the system, which makes it cost quite a pretty penny.

- Double-blind

This is a step-up on the blind test. The double-blind test is a kind of test where only a few people within the organization know that the test is being executed. The employees are not told where or when the attack will happen or who will execute it. This kind of test is very useful due to the fact that it gives some very useful insight into the organization's security monitoring, as well as the efficiency at which the employees execute the instructed procedures.

- Black box testing

This penetration test requires the tester to have no information on the target. It is another variation of the blind test. The tester is instructed to act like an actual attacker and has to find their own entry point and deduce which techniques and tools should be used for the job.

- White box testing

White box testing gives the testers great insight into the important information about the system of the company that they are hired to attack. This information can go anywhere from the IP addresses, to the source code, to the infrastructure schematics. The information provided can be flexible depending on the needs of the company.

It is important for every penetration testing team to use different kinds of tests in order to find all of the weaknesses they can. This, in turn, tells them which kinds of attacks could deal the most damage to the system.

Using different pen testing strategies helps pen testing teams focus on the desired systems and gain insight into the types of attacks that are most threatening.

Penetration Testing Cloud-based Applications

As I have mentioned before, due to the growth of cloud storage, many companies have been moving their infrastructures from on-premise to cloud storage. Due to how cloud itself works, white hat hackers had to develop new techniques and discover some new and interesting angles when approaching penetration testing. The problem with applications that run in the cloud is the fact that there are several obstacles when it comes to pen testing. Both legal and technical problems might occur when you are aiming to check the security of the application. Here is how you, as a beginner, should approach white hat hacking on cloud.

Step 1: Make sure to understand how the cloud provider's policies work

As we know, there are private and public clouds. We will focus on the public side today, as they have their own policies when it comes to penetration testing. A white hat hacker will always have to wait for the confirmation of the provider before executing the test. This puts many limitations on what can be done as a part of the process. To be more precise, whenever you want to pen test an application that is running on a public cloud, you need to do a great deal of research as to which techniques are recommended and allowed by the provider. If you do not follow the procedures that the provider has set, you can get in a load of trouble. For example, your test can sometimes seem like an actual attack which can result in your account being permanently shut down.

Any anomaly in a cloud will be spotted by the provider, who looks for anomalies constantly. Sometimes you might receive a call from someone to check what is going on. More often, however, you will be met with a line of automated procedures that will shut the system down if your actions are perceived as an attack. This can lead to several bad things, like all of your cloud-stored systems and data going offline and you having a lot to explain to your provider before they bring them back online.

Another thing that can happen if you conduct your penetration tests irresponsibly is that you run the risk of affecting other users. There is always the possibility that you will put a load on the resources used by other users while you are pen testing. This is a problem with public clouds, as there are always multiple active users, so not all of the system can be dedicated to one user. This can lead to outrage from the provider, too. They might call you in a not-so-friendly manner or just shut down your account.

To make a long story short, there are rules when you want to poke around public clouds. You will have to keep the legal requirements in mind, along with all of the procedures and policies that the provider instructs you to. If you do not do this, you will face some headaches.

Step 2: Come in with a plan

Whenever you want to run a penetration test on a cloud, you need to come in with a plan. In your plan you are going to have to cover:

- Application(s): Get acquainted with APIs and user interfaces

- Data access: Understand how the data will react to the test

- Network access: Understand how the data and the

application are protected by the system

- Virtualization: Make sure to measure how your workload will be handled by virtual machines

- Compliance: Get acquainted with the regulations and laws that you will have to respect while running the penetration test.

- Automation: Select which tools you will be using while executing the penetration tests

- Approach: See which admins you will involve in the pen testing. There are benefits to not notifying the admins. This gives insight into how the admins would react during an actual attack. This approach is highly resented by most admins.

If you are working as part of a team, you should plan the approach together with the rest of the team and make sure that everyone will follow every part of the plan. The entire team should make sure to not stray away from it, as it could result in all of your efforts being for nothing due to the admin killing your access to the system.

Step 3: Pick out which tools you will use

The market provides you with many tools that can be used in penetration testing. In the past, pen testing on clouds was done via on-premise tools. Recently, however, many tools were made that are specially used for cloud pen testing and will prove to be a cheaper option. Another benefit of these tools is the fact that they leave a small hardware footprint.

What you need to know about these tools is the fact that they simulate actual attacks. There are many automated processes which can pick out vulnerabilities in a system. Hackers have done automated activities like guessing passwords and looking for APIs in order to get into a system. Your job is to simulate these activities.

Sometimes, these tools cannot do everything you might need them to do. Your last resort is usually to write a penetration system of your own. This should always be avoided as much as possible as it could set you back quite a bit.

Step 4: Observe the response

While you are running a penetration test, you will have to keep a close eye on:

- Human response - When it comes to cloud penetration testing, you will always have to track how the admins and users will react to your test. Many will immediately shut the system down in order to avoid damage done to it. Other admins will first try to diagnose the situation in order to identify the threat and the solution to anything similar. You should also keep a close eye on how people react in your client provider.

- Automated response - The first thing you should look at is how the system itself will react to your penetration test. Thee system will spot you and react to you. These reactions can range anywhere from a block of an IP address to your whole system being shut down. No matter how this goes down you need to alert admins that are in charge of applications and security in order to see what actions they took and what happened in their areas.

Both of these responses need to be documented. Once you document your findings and take them into consideration, you will finally see where the weaknesses in the system are and how secure the system is.

Step 5: Find and eliminate vulnerabilities

The final product of penetration testing is a list of vulnerabilities that the team has spotted. There can be a vast amount of issues, while sometimes there can be few or none. If you find none, you might have to run another test in order to re-evaluate the results of the previous one.

The vulnerabilities you might find in penetration tests of cloud applications will usually look similar to the following:

Access application data allowed using xxxxx API.

- API access granted after 20 attempts.

- Password generator detected during access of an

application.

- Encryptions do not comply with regulations.

The issues will almost always be different depending on which application you are testing and what kind of test you executed.

Do not forget that there are different layers to the test. All of the parts like network, storage system, database, etc. are all tested separately. The issues, in turn, are also reported separately. You should always run a test with all of the layers together in order to see how they interact. It is always wise to report what happened in each layer.

You need to keep your cloud provider involved every step of the way in order to avoid any policy or legal issues that might occur due to your penetration test. This will also help you determine which approach is optimal and how it should be applied to the different applications. Most providers will have recommended procedures that will result in the most accurate results on their networks.

General Advice on Cloud Pen Testing

Another thing you should keep in mind is who is on the penetration team. If you are running this in-house, you will always have to assume that not everything has been found. Testing teams that come from within the company will usually leave some room for oversight. They know too much about the applications from the start and might always miss some things that they don't think are worth looking at. White hat hackers are the safer method, though a bit more expensive. They will search through your system more efficiently and in great detail.

Always make sure to see which practices are the most efficient with your provider, as well as which applications you will test and which requirements need to be met with the pen test. Using proven approaches is usually a good way to start.

Penetration testing is more important now than it was ever before. It is the only way to make sure that the things you have on the cloud are as secure as possible in order to accommodate for as many users as possible.

Pen testing is not an option these days. It's the only way to prove that your cloud-based applications and data are secure enough to allow the maximum amount of user access with the minimum amount of risk.

How Do On-premises Security and Cloud Security Compare?

This is a big question for many people. People often write off cloud and immediately assume that saving your data on servers inside of an office is the more secure option. This is usually the case due to the fact that you own the hardware and software when you store your data on-premises. This, however, can be detrimental due to the fact that some of the best cloud providers can give you a great deal of security that you might not get on-premises.

To be clear, the cloud system is impressive due to the fact that it is made to give 99.99 percent durability and make everything stored available all of the time. This kind of availability can not be replicated on premise due to the limitations of the hardware and software that is available to you. In order to recreate these results, it would take a huge investment and a huge number of people to manage.

Before being quick to decide which option you are going to go for you need to consider a lot of things. You need to take your budget and how big your security team is into consideration. If your answer seems to be lacking, remember that cloud providers have large teams that will deal with these things for you and have automated systems that constantly protect the system. To make a long story short, cloud companies have dedicated a large amount of time and money to make their systems what they are and it makes them much more reliable.

Chapter 8: Most Common Security Tools

The market for security tools is as extensive as the field itself. In order to separate the hundreds of different tools, it helps to split them up into different categories.

The first category are event managers. These tools respond to events that are happening on the networks you are monitoring. They analyze the logs on your systems in order to detect these events.

Another useful kind of tool is packet sniffers which help you decode packages while digging into the traffic in order to scan their payload. Packet sniffers are used when you go deeper into security events that are happening.

Intrusion detection and prevention systems are another useful category of tools. They might sound similar to firewalls and antiviruses, but they differ in function greatly. When it comes to this software, you should always think of them as a perimeter around your network which is there to spot any unauthorized activity.

Of course, not every tool can be classified into a category due to how specific they are when it comes to function and design. They, however, can be very useful for a lot of different situations.

It is very hard to determine which tools are better than others in different categories due to the different purposes they might have. Most of the tools that we are about to talk about are vastly different from one another and you can never say that one is definitely better than another. This means that it is hard to select tools for each different job, but here are some widely used tools that you should always take into consideration when you are going into a job.

SolarWinds Log and Event Manager

You might not have heard about SolarWinds before, but you should listen closely now. This company has made a vast amount of useful administration tools over a number of years. In the NetFlow collector and analyzer market, SolarWinds's NetFlow Traffic Analyzer is a widely-loved tool. Another great tool that SolarWinds has given us is the Network Performance Monitor, one of the best in the market for SNMP network monitoring tools. To keep it short, the thing that you should know about SolarWinds is that they offer a wide variety of free tools that you can use for different jobs and can fulfill many different roles that you might find yourself trying to fill out. Network and system administrators are often grateful to have SolarWinds, as it is a great source of useful tools.

SolarWinds Log and Event Manager Screenshot

When we are talking about SolarWinds, it is hard to ignore some of their greatest pieces of software. If you are looking for network security tools you will first want to check out the LEM, short for Log and Event Manager. This is a simple choice when you are looking for a Security and Event manager system that is very beginner friendly. This is the tool that you want to start with. In the entry-level SIEM market, it is perhaps the most competitive option. When you are dealing with SolarWinds, you can expect to get everything that any basic system would have and something more. The SolarWinds LEM coms with a great log management feature and runs on an impressive engine.

The LEM will also provide you with impressive response features. It spots threats in real-time and is very reliable at what it does. The tool works great when you are trying to protect yourself from zero-day exploits and threats that you do not know anything about due to the fact that it is not based on signature making. Behavior is what this tool is looking for. You will rarely need to update it. One of the best assets of the LEM is the dashboard. The system is very simple and makes short work of finding anomalies and reporting them.

If you are looking to buy the SolarWinds LEM you need to be ready to pay 4,585 US dollars. If you are unsure about the purchase there is always the 30-day trial that the company offers.

SolarWinds Network Configuration Manager

The LEM is not the only impressive piece of software that SolarWinds can boast. They have several other tools that are focused on network security. One of them is their Network Configuration Manager which is used to keep watch over your equipment and make sure that all of it is configured based on certain standards. What it does for your security is that it spots unauthorized changes in your system. This is useful due to the fact that these changes can be a great sign of a pending attack.

The main function of this software is that it helps you recover by restoring your system to the last configurations that were authorized. It also points out the changes and keeps the information in a configuration file. Another thing that it helps you out with is compliance. It helps you pass audits due to the standardized reports that it makes while working.

The Network Configuration Manager comes at a price of 2,895 US dollars. The price can change depending on the managed nodes that you select. This software, like the one before, comes with a 30-day trial if you are unsure about purchasing it.

SolarWinds User Device Tracker

This is another one of the amazing tools that SolarWinds offers. It is a great tool that anyone working in computer security should have. It tracks endpoint devices and users in order to improve your security. You can use it in order to identify which ports are being used and which are available.

This tool is great in situations where you are expecting an attack with a specific target. The tools helps you by pinpointing where the user that shows suspicious activity is. The searches conducted through this software are based on username, IP/MAC addresses, and hostnames. The search can go a bit deeper and go as far as scanning previous connections of the suspect.

The starting price of the User Device Tracker starts out at 1,895 US dollars. It, again, changes based on how many ports the system needs to track. Like the previous programs, this one comes with a 30-day trial as well.

Wireshark

When talking about Wireshark, it would be offensive to say that it is just a security tool. This tool is widely loved and used. It is hailed to be one of the best capture and analysis packages. This tool is used to analyze network traffic in great depth. It can capture and decode any package so that you can inspect the data they contain.

Wireshark has accumulated a great reputation. Due to the quality of service that it provides, it has pretty much become the standard for the other tools in the market. The competition always tries to emulate it as much as possible. Many administrators use the Wireshark in order to check the captures that they got through other software. This was done so commonly that the newer versions of the software will offer you the option to, upon set-up, run a capture file that you already have in order to immediately start going through traffic. Where the tool shines the most is the filters that it comes with. They are a great addition, as they help you point out the exact data that is relevant to you.

The software is hard to get used to. There are courses that run across multiple days that give instructions on using it. Despite that, it is worth learning how to use Wireshark. It is an extremely valuable tool to any administrator. The tool is free and can be used on most operating systems. You can get your own on the official website.

Nessus Professional

Among solutions for identifying malware, issues, and vulnerabilities, the Nessus Professional is one of the most used.

Millions of professionals use the Nessus Professional due to the view from the outside that it provides them with. It also gives you a great deal of insight into how you can improve the security of your system.

The Nessus Professional gives one of the most broad coverages when it comes to threats. It employs a great deal of impressive intelligence and is very easy to use. The software is updated fairly often as well, which means that you will never have troubles with never-before-seen problems. It has a fairly extensive package when it comes to vulnerability scanning.

If you want to employ the services of the Nessus Professional you will have to pay 2,190 US dollars a year. If you are not sure about making the investment, you can make use of the 7-day trial.

Snort

Among open-source IDSs, Snort stands out among the best. This intrusion detection system was made in 1998. It fell into the ownership of the Cisco System in 2013. Snort entered the Open Source Hall of Fame in 2009. This means that it has been recognized as one of the greatest open source software ever. This speaks volumes.

There are three modes of operation in the snort: sniffer, packet logger, and network intrusion detection. The sniffer mode is the basic mode of operation and its main function is reading network packets and showing their contents. The packet logger is fairly similar, except for the fact that the scanned packets are logged onto the disk. The most interesting mode is the intrusion detection mode. It analyzes traffic as instructed by a ruleset that was set by you. Based on what kind of threat it found, you can go through several different lines of action.

Snort can find many different kinds of cracks in the system that can be a sign of a potential attack that can happen in the future. Snort has a website from which you can download it.

TCPdump

If you were ever interested in which packet sniffer was the first, look no further than Tcpdump. The first release of the software was in 1987. Ever since then, it has been regularly updated and maintained. However, the core of the software always stayed the same. Most Unix-like systems come with TCPdump pre-installed, as it is the standard tool for those operating systems.

The default way of functioning for the TCPdump is capturing the traffic in dumps on the screen. You might notice that this is fairly similar to the sniffer mode we talked about before. DUmps can be piped in order to capture specific files for further analysis, similar to the packer logger mode. Wireshark is usually used in tandem with TCPdump.

The greatest strength of the TCPdump is the fact that it easily captures filters and makes use of several Unix commands in order to make the work far shorter and easier. If you have a good knowledge of the Unix-like systems it will not be a problem for you to deal with traffic and capture the specific parts you are interested in.

Kismet

There is a lot to be said about Kismet. It is an intrusion detection system, packet sniffer, and network detector all in one. Its preferred function is when you are working on LAN. It works with most wireless cards and can go through many different kinds of traffic. This tool is compatible with Linux, OS X, OpenBSD, NetBSD, and FreeBSD. The Kismet has very limited support for Windows systems due to the fact that very few network adapters support Kismet's monitoring mode.

This software is licensed under the Gnu GPL License. The way that it differs from other wireless network detectors lies in the fact that the work it does is done passively. It does not make use of loggable packets, but directly detects the presence of access points. It also makes connections between them. Among open-source wireless network monitoring tools, it is the most used.

Nikto

Nikto is another piece of excellent open-source software. It is one of the most popular web server scanners. Its main function is running web servers through a huge number of tests in order to find traces of several thousands of different programs that can be threatening for your security. It can work through different versions of a lot of different servers. It checks the server configurations and checks for anomalies in the system.

Nikto is designed for speed rather than stealth. It will test a web server in the quickest time possible but its passage will show up in log files and be detected by intrusion detection and prevention systems.

Nikto is licensed under the GNU GPL. It can be downloaded from its home on GitHub.

OpenVAS

The OpenVAS, also known as the Open Vulnerability Assessment System, is a set of tools that give a great deal of extensive vulnerability scanning. Most of the components of the system are open-source and the software is completely free.

OpenVAS has two primary components. The first component of the software is the scanner. It, as the name suggests, is responsible for scanning the computers. The manager is the second component. The manager works as a controller for the scanner and works with the results of the scans. The Network Vulnerability Tests database is an additional component that you can add to the software to make it more efficient. You can download the software from two softwares: the Greenborne Security Feed and Greenborne Community Feed. The latter one is free while the first one is paid.

OSSEC

OSSEC stands for Open Source SECurity. It is a host-based program which is used for intrusion detection. This kind of detection system is different from the network-based counterparts due to the fact that the host itself runs the program. Trend Micro owns OSSEC. In the IT security field, this name has quite a bit of weight.

The primary usage of this software is in Unix-like software where its work is dedicated to scanning configuration and files. It sees some usage on Windows systems too, where it keeps an eye on the registry. The tool alerts you via the console or email whenever something suspicious is detected.

OSSEC has a relatively big drawback, just like any other host-based IDS. You have to install a new instance on every device that you are looking to protect. This is mitigated somewhat due to the fact that the information can be funneled to a centralized console.

OSSEC is also licensed under the GNU GPL. If you want to use it, you can download it from the website.

OSSEC is also distributed under the GNU GPL license and it can be downloaded from its own website.

Nexpose

Nexpose is another widely-used tool. It is made by Rapid7 and is used for managing vulnerabilities. It does all of the things a vulnerability manager can. It fulfils the so-called vulnerability manager lifecycle. This means that the software deals with all of the phases that are involved in the process.

When it comes to the features that it comes with, it is a complete whole. There are many interesting features to the software like the virtual scanning option and dynamic discovery. It can scan many different kinds of environments and can handle a number of IP addresses. It is a software in development and is constantly growing.

There are two versions of the product that you can get. There is a community edition which has way less features than the full commercial versions whose prices start at 2,000 US dollars a year. If you have any questions about the software or are looking to download Nexpose, visit the official website.

GFI LanGuard

The GFI LanGuard is hailed as an excellent IT security tool for businesses. This tool was made to help you with scanning networks and automatic patching. It also helps you meet compliance standards. This software is compatible with most operating systems.

GFI LanGuard has a very intuitive dashboard which helps out with identifying viruses as well. It works with web browsers as well. Another strength of the software is the fact that it works with a huge number of different kinds of devices.

If you are looking to purchase the GFI LanGuard, you will notice that there can be a wide variety of different options when it comes to additional features. The price is flexible and is renewed on a yearly basis. If you are not certain about purchasing the software you can try the trial version first.

Security Tools for The Cloud

As I have mentioned before, cloud has become a popular option when it comes to storing software and data due to the fact that it is a very efficient and safe method of keeping your digital valuables safe. The cloud comes with lower costs, easier scaling, and additional mobility. These prospects lead to many businesses moving their data from on-premises to cloud. This, in turn, made hackers more and more inclined to figure out new methods on attacking systems in order to be able to crack clouds. This is why many providers like Dropbox and Evernote give you many different policies that are slowly taking over the business world.

However, the cloud does have flaws of its own. There have been issues regarding data privacy and residency. These issues are, of course, not enough for people to forsake the cloud. This is why there has been a rise on the Interest of cloud-related security as users and providers are always trying to find ways to mitigate some of the risks.

If you are looking to place your business on the cloud, there are a few tools that you should always keep in mind when you want to keep your data safe. However, before talking about them you should first get to know what Shadow IT is.

The term Shadow IT accounts for any systems or services that are used on the data of the organization without the approval of the organization. Shadow IT is nothing new, but it started becoming a rising issue due to the rise of the popularity of the cloud.

This makes it harder for companies to keep their data safe due to the fact that it makes policies harder to implement.

Three out of the following five tools focus on mitigating the security risks that you might run into while dealing with cloud computing.

Bitglass

Bitglass has not been completed yet and is still in beta. It offers protection for the data of your business. Bitglass can be used on both computers and mobile devices. It aims to maintain your data's visibility and reduce the risk of that data being lost on either the device or the cloud itself.

Bitglass covers several types of security due to how much has been combined in this package. When talking about what it can do for cloud applications, Bitglass can do several things. It can detect the usage of the applications and encrypt the data that you have uploaded to the cloud.

Another great thing about Bitglass is the fact that it can track your data no matter where it is on the Internet. This means that you have vision on the data no matter where it goes and in whose hands it is. It also mitigates a great deal of risk when it comes to compromised data due to device loss. Bitglass has the ability to wipe a device of your data without having to take any additional steps.

Skyhigh Networks

Skylight Networks uses logs from firewalls and proxies that already exist in order to analyze and secure your cloud applications. It tracks the usage of the applications from both authorized and unauthorized sources.

You can customize the risk assessment in order to make sure that the results are what you want to see about your system, without any additional unnecessary information. Another great thing Skyhigh can do is detect inconsistencies in your system, as well as data leaks.

The last notable feature of the Skyhigh Networks is that it has 3-Click Security. This means that it can employ policies across the entire cloud and give you direct access to applications without using device agents or VPNs. On top of that, you can use Skyhigh to encrypt data and protect it.

Netskope

Netskope is specifically made with shadow IT in mind. It can monitor cloud apps and discover anomalies on your network. It monitors a wide variety of different activities on your network and will provide you with extensive reports on your analytics and the gathered information.

It will help you out with the questions you might have regarding business and security in order to spot out vulnerabilities in your system.

Another great feature of the Netskope is the policy enforcement that can help you keep an eye on your employees while they interact with applications on the cloud, all while stopping any activity that you might deem to be unwanted. It allows for the employee to increase their productivity, while not hurting your security.

CipherCloud

CipherCloud aims to encrypt and tokenize your data in order to secure your cloud. Unlike the previous few tools, this one does not focus on shadow IT. Rather, it makes sure to make the known parts of the cloud as secure as possible.

CipherCloud is fairly specific due to the fact that the data you upload is encrypted upon upload and decrypted while it is being downloaded. Your business network will maintain the encryption keys that are used in the process. This means that any unauthorized user will just get a batch of unreadable text instead of useful data.

CipherCloud can also detect malware and prevent loss of data. There are several builds for the CipherCloud that are specialized specifically towards helping out specific systems, while there are several that work with any application on the cloud.

Okta

Okta is quite unique among these five solutions for cloud applications. Okta's aim is to make sure that there is a secure SSO, short for Single Sign-On, for all of the applications that your business owns. Okta can interact with most commonly used applications that you might encounter in most businesses.

Okta has many useful features that you will be grateful to have like mobile device support and multifactor authentication.

The software will provide you with detailed audit logs, which means that you will be able to track the access that your users have to your cloud apps. Another great thing is the centralized control panel from which you can control the access policies across the whole system. It gives you the option of role-based administration as well.

Cloud Penetration Testing From the Point of View of the Customer

When it comes to on-premise penetration testing, you would usually assume that you will be the owner of all of the components and that any testing that you do will be done under your supervision and with your approval. In the cloud, penetration testing works a little differently. The major drawback of the cloud is the fact that consumers and providers share the responsibility when it comes to computer security. Both of these groups are eligible to do penetration testing on the applications on the cloud. There are two things that you need to think about when you are looking to do penetration testing on the cloud. The first thing that you need to consider is if you are a consumer or a provider. The other factor is the service model you have selected.

The Responsibilities of Consumers and Providers

Cloud providers have a vast variety of different opportunities when it comes to penetration testing, even the most brutal ones like DDoS testing and red team testing. There is a huge amount of competition when it comes to the cloud service market. There are many giants that provide excellent service and the need to improve is getting more and more overwhelming.

Cloud users have been more and more interested in cybersecurity. They often interact with their providers in order to get more involved in the security process and penetration testing.

The consumers themselves have a much more limited access to applications and penetration testing in the cloud. These restrictions heavily depend on the model that your cloud service provider employs.

Penetration Testing Depending on the Cloud Service Model

There are three different cloud service models: SaaS (software as a service), PaaS (platform as a service), and IaaS (infrastructure as a service). These three models are different from one another due to how responsibilities are divided between the provider and consumer when it comes to cloud layers.

In order to understand these models, you first need to get to know the eight layers of a cloud:

- Facility (buildings).

- Network (both physical and virtual).

- Computers and storage (specifically file storage and hardware supplying CPU).

- Hypervisor (The hypervisor is used in virtualized environments. The job of the hypervisor is handling the allocation of the resources between the machines in the system.).

- Operating system (OS) and Virtual machine (VM) (These two are considered to be in the same layer due to the fact that when it comes to non-virtualized environments the job of running storage hardware falls to the OS, while in virtualized environments the VM is responsible for this job.).

- Solution stack (makes use of databases and programming languages).

- Application (this layer is composed out of the applications used by the users).

- Application program interface (API) or Graphical user interface (GUI) (consumers and customers use this layer to interact with the system).

What you can do with the applications and penetration tests is directly dependent on what kind of control you have over the layers. The different kinds of models give you different extents of control over the layers.

IaaS model

The IaaS model is specific because the control over the OS and virtual machine, as well as the upper cloud levels, falls to the user. The provider is responsible for the connectivity of the hardware and network. This means that consumers are allowed to execute penetration testing on the API/GUI, application, solution stack, and the VM layers.

PaaS model

In the PaaS model, the provider gives all of the software and hardware that is necessary to run an application, while the consumer only deploys the application. This model gives the consumer fewer layers to deal with: the API/GUI and application layers to be exact.

SaaS model

The SaaS model is similar to the PaaS due to which layers can be tested by the consumer and what the provider delivers. The scope of testing is limited to the API/GUI layer. However, some providers that employ this model let their users run their own applications independent of the system. These applications can be tested by the consumer whenever they want.

Things You Should Remember as a Cloud Penetration Testing Customer

There are two golden rules when it comes to penetration testing on the cloud:

- Always ask your provider if you want to run a test

- Run penetration tests only on the layers that you control

Most providers have certain requirements that need to be fulfilled before they allow you to get into their systems. Usually, you can find this information on the website of the provider. If you make any unauthorized penetration test or do testing without meeting the requirements, your account will be shut down because the provider needs to take care of the security of the other users as well so they can not take any risks with suspicious activity.

A provider's job is not an easy one. They always have so many things to think about and balance out. They always have to make sure that the data of their customers is safe, but still leave the interests of the customer unharmed due to the security policies the provider might implement. The provider is not all-powerful, so the penetration testing that they can do must be done within their own domain. It's a good thing that no cloud provider will access your data without your permission, so you can rest easy knowing that your privacy is safe.

Chapter 9: What Do I Need to Know

How do you get a job? What education and experience do you need?

To say that ethical hacking is a job like any other would be highly incorrect. It does not require any kind of diploma or certification. Knowledge and experience are all that matters in this line of work. No matter how many diplomas you have, the most important thing is your resourcefulness and know-how. The certificates can be easy to acquire once you prove yourself.

Do you need any certifications or licenses?

In order to be an ethical hacker, you will not have to have any certificates. It is, however, nice to have them, as they are confirmation of your skill in the field. There are many different certifications whose value depends on the job that you are aiming for. You should do your research when you are aiming for a certification. The most valuable skills you can have in this field of work, other than the knowledge itself, are persistence, communication skills and problem solving.

The Nature of the Work

What lies behind the surface level of the job? What will you be doing most of the time?

If you are doing this line of work, you will get access to some very vulnerable systems. Once you are inside of them, you will notice just how much damage a well-placed attack could do to the system and the corporation itself. You will see the connections they shouldn't have, programs that need patching, if the software and hardware are properly used, and if the passwords stored on the system are safe. Every network is just a mass of interconnected systems that are easier to crack into than it might appear at first. This is especially important with networks that take care of your money or personal information. An important thing that you need to keep in mind is how informed you are. Social networks are a great place to find out some fresh news before it pops up in other mediums.

Most of the time while doing this line of work will be spent on just probing around networks and poking away at potential vulnerabilities and documenting the findings and informing your clients about them. At times you might feel like you are back in school due to the sheer amount of reports that you will make as a hacker. The reports need to be informative and concise, as they are the only insight that your client will have into their systems.

It is important for the client to be involved every step of the way. Even though the process is very open, the client might get lost in all of the little intricacies of the process due to the technical knowledge needed to understand them.

What are the common assumptions that people make about the line of work?

People often connect the word "hacker" with malicious acting people that deal in illegal activities. This, however, as I have said many times, is untrue. Hackers are people that like to explore how new tools and software can be used in order to solve problems and open up new lanes of attacking. The malicious individuals that use their knowledge to hurt people or steal money and information are not hackers. These individuals are mere criminals and nothing more. The hacking community resents the fact that they need to identify as "ethical hackers" due to what kind of reputation the criminals gave the word. The term "cracker" was always a possibility when talking about criminal hackers, but is often overlooked.

Some people like to look at the hacking process and think of it as if it were a magician's performance. On the contrary, hacking is a well devised process that is aimed towards systematically going through a system in order to improve a network or a system. Despite what some people think, hackers are nothing other than people who have great insight into how systems works.

Computers will always do only what they are told and nothing else.

Another wrong assumption people like to make is that every test a white hat runs is the same. Sadly, this field of work is barely explored and penetration testing is fairly unknown to most individuals as a term. There are many different penetration tests that all have a different skill requirement.

How many hours a day are you going to work?

The amount of time you will require to spend daily while working heavily depends on what kind of activity you are partaking in. If a high-end company hired you to run a penetration test, you will have to work 8-10 hours a day. Every job can take up to 10 weeks to complete. If you are just looking around the system or network for vulnerabilities, the amount of time you are going to spend on it depends on you.

If you are called by a company in order to help them recover from a security breach, then your hours might go through the roof. All-nighters are nothing strange for people in this line of work. Stopping an attack from further damaging the system is not an easy task, especially due to the fact that it is your responsibility to control the damage and help the company get back into action.

Are there any tips and shortcuts that can help you out in the job?

Make sure to always keep up with the news. There are always new methods popping up and you might find someone who found an easier way to do something you are interested in. Always keep a documentation of your exploits and the information you gathered in order to keep track of what you have been doing. By doing this you can avoid making yourself feel bad over wasting time or not seeing the solution in time.

Always remember that there is no such thing as too much communication. No hacker has ever been fired due to giving a client too much info about the system. You will rarely find a client that will instruct you to give them less information. Generally, clients like to be informed on what is happening on their system no matter how miniscule it is, and they will usually appreciate the work you put into relaying that information in an understandable fashion.

Are there any things you can do to stand out from the rest of the white hats?

There is a common misconception among companies that an ethical hacker's job is to just scan the system in order to find a vulnerability and that there is nothing more to it. This, however, isn't true. A white hat hacker's job is far more extensive and in-depth. They will always try to figure out why the program is vulnerable and how that vulnerability can be abused by a malicious individual, as well as the actual amount of damage that a successful black hat hacker can cause.

Finding vulnerabilities in a network is fairly easy. The main chunk of work that a hacker needs to do comes from analyzing what the vulnerability means for the system. You might want to know what the hacker could do and would want to do by using that vulnerability, as well as how the vulnerability interferes with other parts of the system. It can also help you figure out how a criminal hacker would go about cracking into the system, preventing any kind of similar attack from being effective.

What about the job is the worst part and how can you deal with things like that?

Few things can throw you off like specific clients. You might sometimes be hired by people who are not really interested in what is going on in their system and are just looking to do it for the sake of doing it. Another kind of client that will cause some substantial stress is the indifferent kind. Some companies are not always happy to hire a white hat hacker to help them out due to the fact that they think that repairing the damage left by the hacker will always be much cheaper than hiring a professional to help them improve the security of their networks. On the other hand, the more unwilling clients might hire a white hat hacker purely out of fear about their system being cracked. This can be compared to when your car starts making weird noises. You will go see a mechanic as soon as possible in order to see if something is wrong.

Some customers might be concerned that the services of a white hat hacker can cost a pretty penny. This is not always the only concern, as people who look for services are often people who rely on their IT skills as a job. If you detect a lot of vulnerabilities and problems, you might make the individual look bad.

The best thing you can do in situations like this is to just keep up the good work. Always do your best and make sure to report everything that you find, as well as what that could mean for the network. Remember, you are not responsible for protecting the system yourself. That responsibility falls on the client himself. The best you can do is hope that they will do right by themselves.

Where is the enjoyment in the job? What makes it so attractive?

It is hard to pinpoint exactly what the best thing about the job is. Some people take great satisfaction in the fact that they are doing something that would be illegal if the situation were any different. People often joke about how they start to think like a criminal after a while. This is true in most cases and can be a fun way to approach the job.

There are many interesting people in the sector. You will always have fun exchanging knowledge and stories from work with them, as well as potentially make new friends.

What might give you the most satisfaction in the job, however, is the fact that you are making a huge impact on someone's life. You are helping them not only feel more secure, but also be more secure. You are influencing someone's life in a very good way and it can be quite rewarding on its own. To be honest, the pay is pretty good, too.

Clients and General Advice

Is there anything that you would like your clients to know before looking for your help?

There are several things that clients should often keep in mind. The first, and perhaps the most important thing you should remember about white hat hackers is the fact that they are not superheroes. They are not capable of solving all of your problems just by swooping in. Sometimes clients like to think that once you get into their system you will make it completely safe and that they can run carefree. This, however, is wishful thinking.

While many white hat hackers would like it to work that way, the reality is a bit harder to swallow. It is important for every client to be realistic. It is up to them to decide which parts of the system are the most important and what kinds of risks are acceptable when it comes to protecting them. It is impossible to make a completely impenetrable system. There is always that one vulnerability that you can't see or a new technique that you could not have possibly accounted for. What this means is that a white hat hacker's job is not done when they find a way to prevent a potential attack. They always need to assess the situation in order to see what can be done in order to prevent some successful attack from getting out of hand.

Nobody can protect themselves from a threat that they do not know exists. This is why there are a few steps that you can take to help out the hacker you hired to make sure that they have done everything that was possible to keep your system safe. Before a hacker does a penetration test, you should always provide them with as much important information on the system as possible.

The penetration test aims to find a part of your system that is vulnerable to attacks and use it to show how much that could impact the system itself. Nobody likes their money gone or their sensitive personal information missing, so you should always act quickly to fix the vulnerability as soon as the hacker discovers it.

Something that all clients should know is that the penetration testing is the easy part. Learning from your mistakes and conducting your business in safer ways is the difficult part.

How much can you make while doing this job?

Well, the first thing to point out is that your expectations will be met most of the time as long as they are reasonable. The second thing that is worth mentioning is that hacking is similar to other lines of work when it comes to how much hard work is rewarded. If you work hard enough and get good enough, you will make quite a pretty penny. If you are looking to start working for a large amount of money immediately after you got a certification or gained extensive knowledge in the field, you are going to work yourself to a pulp. Companies can be quite ruthless when it comes to the amount of work they place on you. You might be forced to travel a lot and work long hours. Some hackers often say that, at this point, sleep is a luxury. If you are aiming to have a substantial amount of money flowing into your pocket while working in a healthy manner, you might have to accumulate years of experience in IT fields and computer security.

How does one advance in this field?

Well, this question is an interesting one. It usually depends on the individual that we are talking about. You will gain new knowledge on a daily basis no matter which key area you work in. While these skills are usually different from one line of work to another, gaining experience is the key to progressing. While doing well on exams and getting fancy certificates might help you out, the most important thing you can have is skill while working.

There is another way to stand out among the people you work with. There are conferences held on a yearly basis. If you conduct interesting research and prove it to be useful, your name might start getting a bit of weight to throw around. The more you involve yourself in these conferences, the higher the chance of your name getting mentioned is.

What do clients tend to overvalue or undervalue?

In most cases, clients do not see how valuable they themselves are to the process itself. They like to think that a good hacker is all you need to keep the bad people away. This, however, is untrue, as the client needs to do most of the work when it comes to keeping himself or herself safe. People are also prone to making excuses as to why they are never going to be hacked. They like to say that their firm is too small or that they have no valuable information that someone might want. This all changes fairly quickly once their systems actually do get hacked.

Another common mistake companies make is when they compare themselves to other companies. Some boardroom talks tend to fall down to this. They feel as if they are wasting money if they spent more on security than another similar company.

What people often overvalue, however are compliance standards. People like to think that if you meet these standards, your system is completely safe and nothing wrong can happen when a hacker tries to get into it. What you need to understand about compliance standards is that they are not representative of the performance needed to keep your system secure. They are a rough outline of the absolute minimum in order to not be fined. In order to truly be safe, you will need to go leagues and miles beyond what the compliance standards dictate.

What is the most important thing to remember?

You need to put your heart and soul into it. This is a market that just keeps growing and it is hungry for individuals that are interested in playing around with systems and seeing what makes them tick and how to keep them ticking on.

Make sure to enjoy the process of learning. If it looks like a drag to learn the skills you already know over and over again, then some of the less glamorous parts of the job will surely bore you. You should never stop hoping, though. It is easy to find some specific kind of job that is fun for you and makes you feel fulfilled.

Conclusion

White hat hacking is not something new. In fact, it has been here for a long time, just under different names or under no name at all. There has been a great deal of controversy surrounding white hat hacking for a very long time. Ever since cybercrime started being a common practice among criminals, the word "hacker" has been steadily gaining a malicious reputation. Due to how far computer technology has evolved over a relatively short period of time, it is natural for information to be moved from a physical form to a digital form. There are many criminal organizations that value information over anything so it is natural for them to always find new ways to invade systems. This means that it is more important than ever to have secure systems. Valuable data like passwords that we use every day are something very valuable and that we need to protect.

White hat hacking came as a not-so-obvious solution to finding new ways to protect our systems. Think of a system as if it was a human being. When a person gets sick their body gets weaker and they suffer some damage. However, long-term, if the body gets through the disease, it will get more resilient to the disease in the future. The same can be said for injuries. If you break a bone in one place multiple times over a period of time, the new tissue that will replace the damage will be more resilient than ever before. White hat hacking works on a similar principle. In order to make sure that your system is secure you need to pad out as many vulnerabilities as possible. It is hard to tell where these vulnerabilities are if they are not exploited. However, you can't really wait for an attack to happen in order to spot the vulnerability and hope for the best. Once a malicious hacker gets into your system, there is no telling how far they will go or what they will do. Still, it was necessary to have a method that would help organizations keep their systems up to date with the most recent hacking tools and techniques in order to create countermeasures.

White hat hacking is the only real way to do this. To make the system less vulnerable to a hacker attack is to expose it to danger. This is not something you would trust anyone to do, as it is an extremely precise and delicate process. The professionals you hire to do this for you have to be meticulous in their work and have extensive knowledge of computers.

The problem with being a white hat hacker is that many people automatically make a correlation between you and malicious individuals that do the same activities as you but for different reasons. The calling of hacker is not considered a bad thing everywhere though. People in the IT sector have great respect for certified white hat hackers as it means that they are people that have a huge amount of knowledge in the field and that they use that knowledge to do good for other people. The people who look at white hats as if they are criminals usually do not know what white hats actually do and just focus on the hacker part of the title. This is mainly why white hats do not flaunt the calling and prefer to keep it off of their CVs.

White hat hackers are, however, a force for good. They use the same methods as crackers but do so with the permission of the owner of the system they are hacking into and do so in order to improve the security of the system. The point is that they are the polar opposite of black hat hackers as they make their jobs much more difficult.

The field of white hat hacking has been growing rapidly. This is in great part due to how much cybercrimes have grown over the past several decades, so there are always companies that are looking to hire a good white hat hacker. They are ready to pay a large amount of money but will drain you of your time and energy as it is more than a full-time job. Luckily, freelancing as a white hat hacker is always an option. This road is a bit slower but will take you to more favorable results. As I have mentioned before, the job only requires knowledge and experience, so working hard is the key to success. If you manage to prove yourself in the field, you will rarely have your hands free. You can get several certificates to prove your expertise in the field, but, again, this is not necessary as all you need to do to get a good job is to prove yourself to the employer. After that, it is smooth sailing.

The job might not be for everyone, however. At times, you might be stuck doing the same thing over and over again over a prolonged period of time and that is just not interesting to some people. On the other hand, you will find the line of work extremely interesting if you like learning new things, as new methods are discovered all the time. The job takes a great amount of flexibility, as nothing you do will exactly be done by the textbook. Most of the time you will just be thinking as a cracker in order to get into the system, but before that, there is a phase where you must meticulously gather data on the system. The fun part starts when you actually get to dig into the system. You will poke around to find some weaknesses and then follow a hacking plan in order to determine what kind of damage a malicious user could do from that point. During all of this, you will have to do the thing that so many people dread: making reports.

Reports are the most important result of penetration testing, as they are the direct connection between the employer and the hacker. The reports give a run-down on what the vulnerabilities are, how they can be exploited, and how they can be fixed. A client needs this information in order to determine what needs to be done down the line to ensure that the vulnerability will never be exploited by a malicious individual.

Being a relatively new field, hacking has great promise for creators and explorers. People who are the most renowned in the community are people who develop tools and methods that white hat hackers can use to be more efficient at what they do. Making one of these tools takes a large amount of money and time, so this is a job for only the bravest and the most skilled.

Always remember that, no matter what the media tells you, not all hackers are evil. There are those who use their technical knowledge to take advantage of other people for their own benefit, but white hat efforts are dedicated to stopping this. There are many skilled individuals in the line of work whose names themselves speak volumes.

In this day and age, white-hat hacking has become a necessity if you want your systems to stay safe. Hiring a white hat hacker might put you back a pretty penny at times, but it is well worth it if you have any sensitive or classified data that you don't want to be stolen or destroyed.

Some people underestimate the importance of computer security, saying things like: "It won't happen to me because I do not have any useful data," or "The chances are too low." These people realize the mistake when it's too late and they have already been hacked. You should always stay on top of your computer security, as you never know what could happen and when you can be attacked.

Always remember to stay safe while doing anything with your system. Your data might not be valuable to a hacker, but it is valuable to you and you should not let it be lost.

CPSIA information can be obtained
at www.ICGtesting.com
Printed in the USA
LVHW081726210121
677109LV00043B/1251

9 781801 091466